ETHICS FOR SCHOOL BUSINESS OFFICIALS

William T. Hartman
Jacqueline A. Stefkovich

Published in partnership with the
Association of School Business Officials International

Rowman & Littlefield Education
Lanham • Boulder • New York • Toronto • Plymouth, UK

This title was originally published by ScarecrowEducation.
First Rowman & Littlefield Education edition 2008.

Published in the United States of America
by Rowman & Littlefield Education
A Division of Rowman & Littlefield Publishers, Inc.
A wholly owned subsidiary of The Rowman & Littlefield Publishing Group, Inc.
4501 Forbes Boulevard, Suite 200, Lanham, Maryland 20706
www.rowmaneducation.com

PO Box 317
Oxford
OX2 9RU, UK

British Library Cataloguing in Publication Information Available

Library of Congress Cataloging-in-Publication Data

Hartman, William T.
  Ethics for school business officials / William T. Hartman, Jacqueline A. Stefkovich.
    p. cm.
  "Published in partnership with the Association of School Business Officials
International."
  Includes bibliographical references and index.
  ISBN: 978-1-57886-205-4
  ISBN: 1-57886-205-1

  1. School business administrators—Professional ethics—Pennsylvania—Case studies.
2. Public schools—Business management—Moral and ethical aspects—
Pennsylvania—Case studies. I. Stefkovich, Jacqueline Anne, 1947– II. Title.

LB2823.5.H37 2005
371.2'06—dc22   2004021562

Manufactured in the United States of America.

CONTENTS

TABLES

PREFACE

As a result of their position and their many responsibilities, school business officials (SBOs) often encounter ethical dilemmas involving financial, personnel, and professional issues in their school district. It is crucial that they understand what ethical behavior is, demonstrate that behavior when faced with ethical dilemmas in their position, and support the practice of ethical behavior by others in the school district.

PURPOSE OF THIS BOOK

The purpose of this book is twofold. First, it highlights the importance of ethical behavior in the professional life of SBOs. Second, it helps SBOs incorporate ethical considerations into educational decision making. This second goal is accomplished by presenting multiple ethical frameworks for SBOs to consider. These frameworks are in concert with standards issued by the Association of School Business Officials, International, and from the Interstate School Leaders Licensure Consortium. They include models based on what is just and caring, the role of power in making ethical decisions, community expectations, and standards set forth by professional associations.

In this book we explore these models by encouraging SBOs to develop their own personal and professional codes of ethics and then using these frameworks to analyze cases based on real-life dilemmas. This provides an approach to dealing with ethical dilemmas that SBOs may encounter. SBOs are supported in recognizing an ethical dilemma, framing it in alternative ways to understand the perspectives and behaviors of others, selecting an appropriate approach to resolving the ethical dilemma, and implementing an effective action plan to achieve results.

BACKGROUND FOR THE CONCEPT

The idea for this book emerged through an annual in-service program at The Pennsylvania State University for business managers of the state's Lancaster–Lebanon Intermediate Unit 13. Since 1987, William Hartman, professor of school finance at Penn State, has directed this professional development workshop aimed at exploring issues of interest and concern. While the school districts involved are all from one region of Pennsylvania, the intermediate unit is quite diverse in size, wealth, student demographics, and type of district (urban/suburban/rural). Additionally, there is a large variation in the SBOs' range of experience, including senior, very experienced managers, those in their middle years of experience, and new SBOs.

The 2002 program included a session on ethics presented by Jacqueline Stefkovich, one of the authors of this book, and a colleague of Dr. Hartman's at Penn State. Dr. Stefkovich has worked for over ten years providing pre-service and in-service programs for school administrators on ethical issues, but this was the first time her efforts focused on ethical issues aimed at school business officials.

Participants showed a strongly positive response to the concepts and approaches used and, in the course of this experience, were able to identify many ethical dilemmas they had faced. This session was so well received that in 2003 the authors presented another ethics session, built on the interest generated the previous year. It focused on IU 13 SBOs developing their own cases describing ethical dilemmas they had faced, scenarios that ultimately formed the core of cases presented in this book. In addition, the authors presented an overview of their work at the annual conference of the Association of School Business Officials, International, where they received helpful feedback that was instrumental in conceptualizing and rethinking their initial approach to the book.

ACKNOWLEDGMENTS

The authors wish to thank the business managers of Lancaster–Lebanon IU 13, who worked on this book with us. Their enthusiasm, insights, and helpful criticism are very much appreciated. In particular we want to acknowledge the authors of the cases included in the book: Peggy Hartman, Timothy Shrom, Darcy Brenner-Smith, Gwen Boltz, George Ioannidis, Kurt Phillips, Terry Sweigert, and Laura Cowburn. However, it should be noted that the school districts and characters in the cases have been disguised and, in some situations, modified to fit the case study format. Consequently, readers should not infer that specific incidents in any of the cases are related to a particular school district or individual.

We would like to express our appreciation to Peggy Hartman for her careful, thorough attention in reviewing, editing, and refining the manuscript.

In addition many thanks go to our graduate assistants who worked so diligently to help us with this book: Katherine Heeren, Todd Hosterman, and Robert Griggs. Finally, a special note of gratitude goes to Judy Leonard, staff assistant for Penn State's Education Policy Studies Department, who helped us with numerous revisions.

Part I

UNDERSTANDING ETHICS

Part I of this book contains five chapters that provide the reader with background on understanding basic ethical concepts and how to apply them. Chapter 1 identifies compelling arguments as to why understanding ethics and making ethical decisions is important to all education professionals, especially school business officials. Chapter 2 describes five ethical frameworks, which provide a structure for understanding ethical dilemmas. Chapter 3 looks at professional codes aimed specifically at the work of financial officers in schools. Chapter 4 discusses the importance of professional educators examining their own professional and personal codes of ethics. Chapter 5 defines an ethical dilemma and lays out a four-step model process for dealing with ethical dilemmas in light of the various ethical frameworks. An authentic dilemma is then presented, along with an analysis of the problem, to illustrate the application of the process.

1

ETHICS AND SCHOOL
BUSINESS OFFICIALS

Ethical behavior is generally expected of people in public life, with some glaring exceptions from used car dealers, politicians, celebrities, rock musicians, and sports figures. In recent years, some CEOs and other senior management officials in major corporations have been added to this hall of shame. However, people in education, including SBOs, have always been held to a higher standard.

In the business field in general, there is a strong and growing national concern about the lack of ethical behavior among executives, particularly in regard to finances. Scandals involving an increasing number of major corporations and their senior executives, along with their betrayal of public and stockholder trust for personal greed, have shocked the country. The scandals were heightened because in many cases they were accomplished with the compliance and active assistance of major accounting firms, whose explicit role was to serve as a watchdog against illegal and unethical behavior. Seeing the sordid reports in the media has made the public more sensitive to and cynical about behavior of those in senior management positions.

This national attitude has carried over to education as well. Accountability has become a key and in many cases dominant concept, both internally by educators and externally by politicians, policymakers, and the public. However, accountability is a slippery concept in terms of its meaning and its implementation. Regardless of the difficulties, powerful external groups are using the concept of accountability to examine and question both educational results and educational spending.

In spite of well-documented limitations, student test score results serve as a shorthand measure of accountability. Many states have enacted academic standards in an attempt to increase student achievement. At the national level, the passage and implementation of the federal No Child Left Behind Act (NCLB) legislation requires substantially more testing of students, demonstration of "adequate yearly progress" by all students and by each of identified minority groups, and widespread dissemination of school level results.

To be effective, standards should have a positive educational purpose as well as a motivating one. Standards should be based on what educators and policymakers want students to learn, and they should be able to measure student achievement against those goals accurately and reliably. The use of student test scores on a single annual test to determine and identify publicly which schools are "failing" creates an atmosphere that emphasizes only one aspect of schooling and puts enormous pressure on schools to achieve acceptable test scores by whatever means are feasible. Some of these means, such as improved instructional practices, may be very beneficial, but others could involve school officials with difficult and potentially ethical dilemmas about how to achieve the demanded results.

The demands placed on education are made more difficult because education is a complex enterprise; it is not susceptible to simple solutions that may be imposed by politicians or have been practiced in other sectors. It has many different and sometimes conflicting goals, which are both educational and social. It serves a wide variety of students and communities that differ greatly in their interest in and ability to provide educational programs. The governance structure generally involves elected officials overseeing professionals who carry out the work of the organization. There are no simple, comprehensive ways to measure its results adequately and appropriately, such as quarterly earnings in the private sector.

In spite of the important role education has in the agendas of national and state political leaders, the new mandates and obligations placed on education have largely come without adequate new resources to implement required programs and services. To justify the lack of additional funding to support the newly mandated programs, critics claim that educational spending is bloated and inefficient. This is largely a rhetorical and political stance and one that is unfounded in most school districts. Unfortunately, unfunded mandates, such as increased, more inclusive academic testing, new security measures, rising health costs, and more stringent safety codes, have placed substantial additional demands on school budgets. When the mandates are coupled with difficult economic conditions, educators are placed under significant pressure to achieve improved results with little or no increase in real resources.

CONTEXT OF ETHICS FOR SCHOOL BUSINESS OFFICIALS

SBOs, as part of the senior management team of a school district, are the chief fiscal officers for school districts. This can be a position of power and influence, as well as great vulnerability. Unlike the superintendent, assistant superintendents for instruction, or school principals, often the SBO is the only member of the senior management team who does not have training as an educator or has not had direct teaching or management experience in schools. To be an effective team member, the SBO must balance the business side of the enterprise and the instructional programs that are the core of the district's mission. There is great potential for conflict when different priorities collide and not all programs can be funded as their advocates would wish.

Because the general public (and even some in education) have a fuzzy understanding of the role and duties of SBOs, they are easily linked to accountants and financial officers in the private sector and then tarred with the same brush of unethical, greedy behavior of those who recently discredited Enron, Arthur Anderson, Adelphia, Tyco, and some mutual fund companies. It can be particularly galling for an SBO to be accused of being antieducation or unethical for calling some program or expenditure into question, when in reality the SBO is keeping the district out of fiscal or even legal difficulty. Consequently, understanding what ethical behavior is, recognizing unethical behavior in oneself and others (superiors, peers, and subordinates), and knowing how to make appropriate decisions when faced with an ethical dilemma are more essential now than ever before.

FIDUCIARY RESPONSIBILITIES

In their role as the senior fiscal official in a school district, SBOs are in charge of large amounts of public funds and have a fiduciary responsibility over these funds. This involves budgeting, collecting taxes and other revenues due the district, monitoring fiscal operations to ensure that the funds are properly protected and utilized, and reporting the financial status of the school district accurately and in accordance with professional standards and state statutes and regulations (Hartman 1999).

Fiduciary responsibility goes beyond expenditures and revenues to include responsibility for all assets belonging to the district. The role of the SBO is not only to protect the district's investment in these items but, in many cases, to ensure their efficient operation. This is not just a business issue, but one that can have significant implications for the resources available to instructional programs. Counting the business office, operations and maintenance, and student transportation, approximately 15–20 percent of the current expenditures of a school district come under the responsibility of the SBO; if food services and debt service are included, the percentage is higher. Money saved through cost reductions in these areas can be reallocated to instructional programs. Supporting and enhancing the educational programs of the district is an important aspect of the SBO's role and calls for a professional approach to managing business administration functions and an awareness of the values inherent in that effort.

TEMPTATIONS

In economic terms, education represents a large market for firms and individuals who supply the goods and services that schools use to operate. This can be seen very clearly at national and state SBO conventions, where massive convention halls are filled with vendors displaying their products and distributing free samples. Purchase decisions represent substantial amounts of money and vendors vigorously compete to sell their goods and services. Since they most often make purchasing decisions for noninstructional areas and manage the purchasing function for the entire district, SBOs routinely interact with a variety of vendors. Given the amount of money involved and the number of individuals who wish to share in the purchases made by school districts, there are many opportunities for unethical or illegal interactions between SBOs and vendors and their representatives. Such behavior rarely occurs, but SBOs must maintain an ongoing ethical approach in the face of structural temptations as they carry out their role. The necessity of an ethical approach (to say nothing of a legal approach) applies to the behavior of not only the SBO but also subordinates and others in the school district who may be improperly influenced in purchase decisions by outsiders.

Business services, the territory of the SBO, is an area that most educators know relatively less about. The intricacies of budget codes, alternatives for refinancing long-term debt, purchasing policies for obtaining bids, and awarding contracts to vendors are generally the province of the SBO and are less open to observation or scrutiny by others. To be sure, there are statutes, regulations, policies, and procedures that direct these activities and audits that monitor their proper implementation. However, it is the ethical stance and subsequent actions of the SBO that set the tone of operations in these areas and ultimately either cause or prevent abuses.

2

MAKING ETHICAL DECISIONS

An ethical structure is necessary as a template against which the SBO can evaluate difficult decisions to see how different possible choices measure up to desirable standards of behavior. This structure is a mental picture of what constitutes ethical behavior, and it provides a guide for action or decision making. However, because the situation is not always clear and unambiguous, some ethical values may be in conflict with one another. Consequently, the approach calls for reflective behavior on the part of the SBO when dealing with an ethical dilemma, rather than a hasty "ready, aim, and fire" approach.

The purpose of reflection is to consider alternative choices and their likely impact in light of what the SBO considers appropriate and sought-after outcomes. This does not mean a paralysis of decision making in which every possible nuance is meditated on while the situation blows up. Rather, it suggests the commonsense approach of considering reasonable choices and their potential outcomes and then selecting the actions or set of actions that are most closely in line with the SBO's ethical values.

ETHICAL FRAMEWORKS

To deal with the complexity of the real world, this chapter presents multiple ethical frameworks for the SBO to consider. Often, particularly in difficult situations, the appropriate decision will depend on the perspective of the individuals involved, and different people may have very different beliefs about what should be done and why. One single framework is not adequate to cover all circumstances. The frameworks represent different values and emphases and may lead to conflicting possible choices or actions. However, they also represent the reality that the SBO must face when trying to act in an ethical manner. These different perspectives include decisions based on what is just and what is caring, as well as considerations of less powerful individuals, community expectations, and standards set forth by professional associations. Much of this discussion is based on *Ethical Leadership and Decision Making in Education*, a book by one of the authors, which proposes an ethical framework for the profession (Shapiro and Stefkovich 2001).

Justice

The ethic of justice is likely the ethic that educators find most familiar because it has the longest history. Generally reinforcing a top-down approach, this ethic provides the basis for our legal system (Starratt 1994). Thus reliance on the law, codified interpretations of the law, regulations, policies, and the like, represent thinking within the justice framework. This framework also goes beyond the law to consider issues of fairness and equality. Following strict interpretations of law rather than the "spirit" of the law, one may experience conflict as to the ethical course of action. The justice framework, in combination with the others, provides guidance in dealing with these complex problems. Other concepts falling under the ethic of justice center on questions related to the greater good for the greater number and maximum benefit analysis (Strike et al. 1998). In other words, there may be times when an SBO must sacrifice the rights of an individual person for the greater good of the student body. The ethic of justice explores this balance.

Care

The ethic of care focuses on compassion and empathy. When the ethic of care is valued, school officials emphasize relationships and connections in the decision-making process. Unlike the ethic of justice, the ethic of care is not associated with a top-down or bureaucratic approach. It focuses more on fostering a nurturing climate in schools and often portrays school personnel as caregivers (Noddings 1992, 2003; Sernak 1998). Care for the individual takes precedence over mechanistically obeying the rules.

Power

The ethic of power has also been referred to as an ethic of critique (Apple 2001). This ethic challenges educators to rethink traditional ideas of law and justice to consider who has the power. Concepts supporting the notion that some groups in our society have historically had more say when it comes to determining what is legal, just, and consequently ethical are key here. Within this framework, one might question who makes the laws and how they apply to a variety of different people. One might also look at laws from the past that are now considered bad law and how they shape notions of right and wrong. A historical example would be the Jim Crow laws of the 1950s that mandated separate facilities based on race. In a current context, one might look to issues of favoritism and cronyism to see if certain groups have consistently benefited or been excluded.

Community

In considering the ethic of the community, one must first ask, Who is the community? Is it the school district's governing board, which purportedly represents community interests, a few vocal parents who make their needs known, or active special interest groups, such as taxpayers or the football boosters club? In the ethic of community, one examines how community influences might affect ethical decision making, in both positive and negative ways. Here the SBO must also consider issues of local politics and how they might influence ethical decisions.

The Profession

The ethic of the profession calls for school leaders to consider professional and personal ethical principles and codes, as well as standards of the profession, individual professional codes, and community interests to create a dynamic model that places the "best interests of the student" as the central focus. Professional decision making and professional judgment, developed by a process of grappling with ethical issues through intense personal introspection, are keys to this concept.

As a first step in acting ethically, the ethic of the profession would expect SBOs to examine their own set of core values, which guide decisions in both professional and personal situations. However, this is easier said than done. While individuals may have an intuitive understanding of their feelings of what is right and wrong, to articulate the basic values that shape and guide their feelings and actions is a much

Table 2.1. Summary of Ethical Frameworks

Framework	Characteristics	In Practice
Justice	Rights and laws Rules and regulations Board policies Fairness Hierarchy	Supports equality Balances rights of the groups with individual rights Asks: What is the legal course of action? What is fair?
Care	Personal connections Compassion Nurturance Nonhierarchical	Focuses on feelings and individual relationships Asks: How can we promote a nurturing, positive school climate?
Power	Power and influence Social class inequities Gender inequities Disabilities Ethnic and racial differences Religious differences	Challenges laws and rules Questions the status quo Considers alternative perspectives and role reversals Resists abuse of authority Asks: Who made the rules?
Community	Community standards Community political influence	Considers both the good and bad aspects of community Asks: Who is the community?
Profession	Personal ethical codes Professional ethical codes Professional association standards Best interests of the student	Looks at clashes between personal and professional codes Asks: What is in the best interests of the student? What is in accordance with professional norms?

more difficult and introspective undertaking. Thus SBOs need to develop their own code of ethics to use in their positions. This comes from a structured process of identifying and prioritizing the most important values held by the SBO.

AN INTEGRATED APPROACH

While each of these frameworks provides an approach to examining ethical decision making, it is important to view them not as competitive but as complementary. They can be seen not only as discrete entities, but also as a whole, an integrated approach to understanding how to make ethical decisions. Thus, for the practicing SBO, these frameworks represent various approaches which, when taken together, assist in tackling difficult ethical problems. Table 2.1 summarizes the frameworks, their characteristics, and how they might be applied to practical situations.

3

ETHICS FOR
SCHOOL BUSINESS OFFICIALS

Just as in business, medicine, and law, ethics is a critical consideration for school business officials who deal with not just money but also the community's trust. As mentioned in chapter 1, the time is ripe for this profession to emphasize the need for ethical behavior, as well as to actively consider how ethical behavior plays out in the everyday work life of the school business official.

Both personally, and especially through their professional organization, the Association of School Business Officials, International (ASBO), school business officials have a history of concern for ethical issues. The organization prescribes a ten-point code of ethics for school administrators. This code begins with the well-being of students as fundamental to all actions and decision making. It stresses principles, such as honesty and integrity, and actions, such as maintaining standards, honoring contracts, obeying laws, and adhering to rules, regulations, and policies (see table 3.1). Underlying this code is the belief that the school administrator must exemplify professional conduct. This expectation applies to contacts in the school, the community, and the profession.

Table 3.1.   Code of Ethics for Educational Administrators

The educational administrator:

1. Makes the well-being of students the fundamental value in all decision making and actions
2. Fulfills professional responsibilities with honesty and integrity
3. Supports the principle of due process and protects the civil and human rights of all individuals
4. Obeys local, state, and national laws and does not knowingly join or support organizations that advocate, directly or indirectly, the overthrow of the government
5. Implements the governing board of education's policies and administrative rules and regulations
6. Pursues appropriate measures to correct those laws, policies, and regulations that are not consistent with sound educational goals
7. Avoids using position for personal gain through political, social, religious, economic, or other influence
8. Accepts academic degrees or professional certification only from duly accredited institutions
9. Maintains the standards and seeks to improve the effectiveness of the profession through research and continuing professional development
10. Honors all contracts until fulfillment or release

Source: ASBO, *Professional Standards*, 2001, p. 26.

ASBO CODE OF ETHICS

As discussed above, school business officials, by the very nature of their position, need to be concerned about ethical issues. Ethics is an integral part of ASBO's *Professional Standards*. This document, which primarily focuses on job functions, describes an ethical context encompassing the totality of the SBO's work experience:

> ASBO considers it vitally important that anyone seeking the position, or any entity preparing or certifying individuals to serve as school business officials, recognize, and demonstrate the importance of ethical conduct. The school business official is expected to model moral, legal, and ethical behavior, and always make decisions and provide input to policymakers with the best interests of the students in mind. ASBO supports and promotes the continuous study of the ethics of the profession and is committed to ensuring the highest standards of conduct among school business officials. (ASBO 2001, p. 7)

ASBO STANDARDS OF CONDUCT

As early as 1970, ASBO had a written code of conduct. Since then, this code has been reviewed and revised several times, with its present version consisting of twenty-one standards divided into three general areas. The first grouping, relationships with the school district, emphasizes supporting the school district's goals, objectives, and image, implementing and interpreting district policies, assisting fellow administrators in fulfilling their obligations, and treating subordinates in a fair and just manner.

The second area, conduct of business and the discharge of responsibilities, stresses honesty and integrity in business dealings and avoidance of actions supporting preferential treatment and/or personal gain. School business officials must avoid situations that may lead to conflict of interest, accepting gifts, or soliciting money for gifts to superiors.

The third focus, relationships with colleagues in other districts and professional associations, includes supporting colleagues' actions and offering assistance when needed. Actively supporting professional associations and assuming leadership roles and responsibilities are encouraged, but "taking over" these associations or using one's involvement in the association for personal gain is considered inappropriate conduct. (See table 3.2 for a complete listing of these standards.)

Table 3.2. Standards of Conduct for School Business Officials

In relationships within the school district it is expected that the school business official will:

1. Support the goals and objectives of the employing school system
2. Interpret the policies and practices of the district to subordinates and to the community fairly and objectively
3. Implement, to the best of the official's ability, the policies and administrative regulations of the district
4. Assist fellow administrators as appropriate in fulfilling their obligations
5. Build the best possible image of the school district
6. Refrain from publicly criticizing board members, administrators, or other employees
7. Help subordinates achieve their maximum potential through fair and just treatment

In the conduct of business and the discharge of responsibilities, the school business official will:

1. Conduct business honestly, openly, and with integrity
2. Avoid conflict of interest situations by not conducting business with a company or firm in which the official or any member of the official's family has a vested interest
3. Avoid preferential treatment of one outside interest group, company, or individual over another
4. Uphold the dignity and decorum of the office in every way
5. Avoid using the position for personal gain
6. Never accept or offer illegal payment for services rendered
7. Refrain from accepting gifts, free services, or anything of value for or because of any act performed or withheld
8. Permit the use of school property only for officially authorized activities
9. Refrain from soliciting contributions from subordinates or outside sources for gifts or donations to a superior

In relationships with colleagues in other districts and professional associations, it is expected that the school business official will:

1. Support the actions of a colleague whenever possible, never publicly criticizing or censuring the official
2. Offer assistance and/or guidance to a colleague when such help is requested or when the need is obvious
3. Actively support appropriate professional associations aimed at improving school business management, and encourage colleagues to do likewise
4. Accept leadership roles and responsibilities when appropriate, but refrain from "taking over" any association
5. Refrain from using any organization or position of leadership in it for personal gain

Source: ASBO, *Professional Standards*, 2001, p. 27.

4

EXAMINING PERSONAL AND PROFESSIONAL CODES OF ETHICS

The Association of School Business Officials (ASBO) provides school business officials with direction regarding proper and ethical behavior. However, all professional codes of ethics, even the best, have limitations and must be interpreted and used appropriately. When professional codes provide detailed guidance, it might be tempting to apply a code as the rule rather than looking to the spirit of the code's mandates and the complexity of the situation. No code, no matter how detailed, can cover all eventualities. Accordingly, while codes of professional ethics provide excellent guidelines for ethical behavior, applying these principles to real situations can be difficult.

To be truly meaningful, professional codes of ethics must be internalized. Thus there is merit in constructing a personal professional code of ethics to see how it meshes with that of the professional association. This book proposes a six-step approach to accomplishing this objective.

This process involves identifying both personal and individual professional codes of ethics, comparing them to each other and then to the ASBO code of ethics. The steps to this process are outlined in table 4.1 and elaborated in the remainder of this chapter.

Table 4.1.   Steps in Examining Personal and Professional Codes of Ethics

Step 1: Identify your personal code of ethics.

Step 2: Articulate your own individual professional code of ethics.

Step 3: Compare and contrast personal and individual professional ethical codes.

Step 4: Reconcile differences between personal and individual professional codes.

Step 5: Compare and contrast your individual professional ethical code with the ASBO code of ethics.

Step 6: Reconcile differences between your individual professional code and the ASBO code of ethics.

STEP 1: IDENTIFYING ONE'S OWN PERSONAL CODE OF ETHICS

Developing a personal code of ethics begins with considering the following questions. They help you identify the values that form the basis for your beliefs and guide your actions.

1. What ethical actions do I privilege?

    In any given situation involving ethical decision making, what do you think of *first*? Some examples might include (but are certainly not limited to) deciding what is fair for the majority, concern for individual rights, consideration of how your actions might affect others, use and abuse of power, community mores, standards of the profession, and the best interests of students.

2. What are the critical incidents in my life that shaped my ethical perspective?

    Here you would consider specific events in your life that shaped later perspectives. Perhaps there was a bout with inequity that made you more in touch with issues of discrimination, an incident where a decision had to be made between caring and upholding a "higher" principle, or a situation that involved abuse of power or conflict of loyalty. Identify these incidents and see where they fit within the various ethical frameworks.

3. What are the moral principles that guide my ethical decision making?

    After reflecting on the questions above, you can develop a personal code of ethics by articulating those things that you hold as moral principles.

Table 4.2.   Example of a Personal Code of Ethics

- Treat others as you would like to be treated.
- Deal honestly with others.
- Be loyal to family and friends.
- Take care of physical well-being; avoid excess.
- Attend to spiritual growth.
- Be happy with what you have; don't envy others.
- Be kind to elderly people.

It is difficult to tell individuals what their personal codes of ethics might look like. For example, a graduate student in educational leadership once asked one of the authors for an example of a personal code of ethics. When the professor was reluctant to provide this template, the student pressed further: "Does it look like the Ten Commandments?"

The answer to the latter question is, It depends. For many people, but not everyone, religion has a profound influence on ethical decision making, but in varying ways. For someone from a Jewish or Christian tradition, the Ten Commandments might well be a driving force behind that person's personal code of ethics. On the other hand, persons who have different, less central views of religion or have been influenced by other experiences and critical incidents may give less importance to the Ten Commandments. Certainly persons grounded in different religions may (or may not) have different perspectives.

Depending on the person, factors such as race, gender, culture, and a myriad of other influences may play an equal or perhaps more important role than religion. In essence, it depends on the individual. A personal code of ethics is just that, personal—deeply personal—and based on serious, sometimes painful reflection. Table 4.2 presents a simple personal code of ethics as an illustration.

STEP 2: ARTICULATING AN INDIVIDUAL PROFESSIONAL CODE OF ETHICS

Once you have developed a personal code of ethics, it is time to articulate an individual professional code of ethics. This is accomplished in much the same manner as the personal code except that it applies to a work situation. First, reflect on your work life and important events that have shaped it. Then, list seven to ten ethical principles that guide this work. Next, prioritize these principles. As with the personal code, a fairly simplistic example of an individual code of professional ethics is provided in table 4.3 as an illustration.

STEP 3: COMPARING AND CONTRASTING PERSONAL AND PROFESSIONAL CODES OF ETHICS

There may be conflicts between personal and professional codes of ethics. Thus any professional code of ethics must be seen in the context of your personal codes of ethics. Step 3 in this process expects professionals to reflect on both their personal code of ethics and their individual professional code of ethics. Here you consider:

- What are the similarities?
- What are the differences?
- Are there clashes between these personal and professional codes of ethics?
- If so, what factors control decision making?

STEP 4: RECONCILING DIFFERENCES BETWEEN PERSONAL AND PROFESSIONAL CODES OF ETHICS

It is vitally important to reconcile any differences that exist between your personal and professional codes of ethics. Since the differences

Table 4.3. Example of an Individual Professional Code of Ethics

- Be loyal to employers.
- Treat others as you would like to be treated.
- Deal honestly with others.
- Be straightforward—frank—with others.
- Always be courteous and kind.
- Act as a role model for other professionals.
- Serve as a mentor for newer professionals.
- Balance time between work, home, and family.

depend on context, this reconciliation may not be difficult in some in-stances. For example, in the illustrations provided in tables 4.2 and 4.3, one might value frankness with others as a good professional practice where money or personnel issues are involved, yet always being straight-forward with others might prove to be a problem in personal situations where a friend or family member's feelings might be easily (and perhaps unnecessarily) hurt.

Sometimes there may be outright conflicts. For instance, if the SBO (as in table 4.2) believes that it is morally right to be loyal to family, then he or she might confront an ethical dilemma if a work situation required compromising a family member's integrity or confidentiality.

STEP 5: COMPARING AND CONTRASTING PROFESSIONAL CODES OF ETHICS

There may be clashes between various professional codes of ethics. For example, as one of our workshop participants pointed out to us, SBOs coming from the business world or wealthier school districts may assume that taking full advantage of an expense account is how business is conducted, while SBOs in poorer districts may experience moral conflict in spending scarce community resources in such a manner, even when the end result benefits the school district.

A good exercise for SBOs is to compare and contrast their individual professional codes with the ASBO code of ethics (presented in chapter 3). Table 4.4 provides some direction.

Table 4.4.   Comparing and Contrasting Professional Codes of Ethics

- Consider the principles in your individual code of ethics in relation to those outlined in the ASBO code of ethics.
- What are the similarities?
- What are the differences?
- Were there items that the ASBO code included that you omitted?
- If so, why did you omit them?
- Were there items you included that were not in the ASBO code? If so, why did you include them?

STEP 6: RECONCILING DIFFERENCES BETWEEN PROFESSIONAL CODES OF ETHICS

If there are differences between your own professional code of ethics and the ASBO code, you need to decide how important these differences are, what the nature of the conflict is, and how to deal with that conflict. For example, if an SBO's individual code of ethics places a high priority on loyalty to an employer, but the employer expects behavior contrary to ASBO code of ethics, this situation presents a serious dilemma for the SBO.

The ultimate decision that a school business official (or any professional) must make is determining lines that cannot be crossed: moral principles that cannot be compromised, even if it means leaving the school district or the community. Fortunately, resolution of most moral dilemmas does not result in such dire consequences, but all school professionals, and especially SBOs, should be prepared to confront these types of issues.

In essence, reflecting on personal and professional codes of ethics, identifying conflicts, and sorting out these conflicts take time. Ultimately, however, this process will provide you with a greater capacity to make sound ethical decisions. To assist this process, chapter 5 provides guidelines for recognizing and dealing with ethical dilemmas and an authentic case involving an SBO facing an ethical situation in his work.

5

APPROACHING ETHICAL DILEMMAS

DEFINITIONS AND CONSIDERATIONS

What exactly is a dilemma? The word comes from Greek and means "ambiguous position." The *New Heritage Dictionary* refers to a dilemma as a predicament that seemingly defies a satisfactory solution. Other pertinent terms are "difficult," "perplexing," or "trying." The saying "between the devil and the deep blue sea" aptly describes many dilemmas.

Ambiguity, one of a dilemma's main features, makes an already difficult situation even more complex and confusing. Something that is ambiguous is susceptible to multiple interpretations. In a dilemma the ambiguous nature comes to the fore; there may be layers of considerations involved and different possible solutions conflict with one another.

An ethical dilemma has a further complication in that it involves differing moral stances. For school business managers, this situation may be characterized by the presence of competing aspects of their own values and with the values of others. The ethical dilemma activates beliefs of right or wrong, good or bad. It brings moral duty or obligations into consideration, and the various parties involved may have strongly held but differing beliefs about the proper course of action.

However, not all dilemmas have ethical overtones—or underpinnings—even though they involve tough decisions and conflicting solutions. If the problem can be resolved satisfactorily by simply applying a law or policy to the situation, it is probably an implementation or enforcement issue, rather than one involving ethical choices.

As illustrated in chapter 2, the five ethical frameworks offer guidance for thinking about and dealing with ethical situations or dilemmas for SBOs. The combination of a personal code of ethics and the multiple frameworks for viewing an ethical dilemma, including the professional dimension, provides SBOs with an approach to dealing with dilemmas they may encounter. The general approach is not complex or difficult to understand, but it can be challenging to put into practice. The basic stages in the process are:

1. Recognizing an ethical dilemma
2. Framing it in alternative ways to understand the perspectives and behaviors of others
3. Selecting an appropriate approach to resolving the ethical dilemma
4. Implementing an effective action plan to achieve results

To illustrate how the process is applied, an ethical dilemma that one SBO faced is presented below, together with an analysis using the multiple frameworks approach. The outcome of the case is also provided. Of course, as is usually the situation with ethical dilemmas, other choices might be made by individuals with other values and perspectives.

In working through an ethical dilemma, much can be gained by initially gathering as much information as possible, attempting to ensure the accuracy of the information and increasing your understanding of the issue. What was it specifically that the school board president said? Who actually attended the meeting? What research has been done in this area? Taking steps to get more facts and clarify the situation, gathering relevant data and, in general, organizing available information can put things into a clearer perspective. The ethical dilemma, if ethical questions remain at the core of the issue, must still be solved, but confusion and misinformation are reduced, and often choices are more evident.

In the case that follows, and in many of the cases presented in part II, one of the first actions the SBO takes is to seek more facts that have a bearing on the situation. In wrestling with the problems confronting them, SBOs need to be as informed as possible. Frequently information leads to different conclusions than originally intended, and many times suggests compromises that can be worked out for a solution.

THE CASE: SEAT BELTS ON SCHOOL BUSES

After a tragic school bus accident in another state, in which two children were killed and several more were seriously injured, a group of parents got together to promote seat belts in school buses in their district. They took their concerns to the superintendent and were invited to speak at the next meeting of the school board.

"Children's lives are at risk," said their spokesman. "We tell them over and over again to buckle up every time they get in the car. In fact, state law requires it! Why do we make an exception for when they ride in the school bus? It makes no sense at all, that they should be airborne objects if there is a sudden stop or, God forbid, an accident."

The chair of the school board turned to Mr. Doyle, the business manager for the district. She asked, "What was it we were told the last time this issue was brought up?" Since he knew this would be on the evening's agenda, Mr. Doyle was prepared. He had with him the school bus manufacturer's safety report, a thick document that he now held up.

"When we visited this problem before, we got as many facts and figures as we could, and this report indicates that safety belts are actually a hindrance, and could even be dangerous, in a school bus–related accident situation. The safety padding in the front and back of the seats is specially designed to cushion impact and is more than adequate. Besides," he went on, "we found out that equipping proper size belts for different age-groups is a real problem, as well as the difficulty of ensuring use. Who will make sure all kids are buckled up? The driver? Suppose kids unbuckle again. Who will be liable?"

The school board chair then addressed the spokesman of the parent group. "We appreciate your concern and you do make an excellent point, particularly about reinforcing seat belt use in the family car, but we have looked, exhaustively, into this subject before. The expenses are overwhelming. The bus company has told us that retrofitting our existing buses would be . . . what was it, Mr. Doyle?"

The business manager consulted his notes. "Over $6,000 per bus, and that was six years ago," he said, "but the bus company clearly stated that retrofitted belts were unreliable and they could not guarantee them. We'd actually need new buses, which could run us into tremendous expense."

A board member then raised her hand to speak. "If I recall, we also learned that side impacts and rollovers were the kind of accidents not protected by padding, and that seat belts are a better protector. I'm suspicious of a report that is prepared by the manufacturer. Remember last winter when one of our buses skidded on the ice? That was a close call. Some kids received nasty bruises."

"Yes, but," countered another member, "they get bruises on the sidewalk when it's icy and they're messing around. I read that children are eight times safer riding in school buses than in family cars, and that accidents are three times more likely to happen when children are boarding or leaving the bus, than when they're riding in it."

"Then why are seat belts being required in all new school buses in Florida?" a third board member asked. "I've been looking into this matter and I think this group of parents is on the right track."

The board's attorney then entered the discussion. "It is the question of liability that is particularly of concern. Someone has to be responsible to ensure that Johnny is buckled up and stays buckled up."

"I agree," said the school board chair. "I don't see how we could enforce seat belt use, even if we could afford the expense. We will, of course, look into the matter, but we have so many other priorities and, given the terrific cost of new buses, I'm afraid other programs would have to be given up or curtailed immensely. I think our money would be better spent on improving instruction and test scores, particularly since there is still a controversy about whether seat belts are even necessary. From what I've read there are only eleven fatalities a year nationally among the millions of kids transported—I think it's over 20 million—and it's the driver who was killed in a quarter of these crashes. As tragic as they are, an accident of that nature is so remote a possibility that I don't see how we can justify the investment."

The parent group could be heard making angry comments. Their spokesman rose to his feet. "Do you mean to tell us that you would compromise our children's safety? Extra padding was not enough to save the lives of the children who were killed! This issue is more important than spending money for computers or anything else! We're not going to take no for an answer." And they stormed out.

The next day, Mr. Doyle groaned as he saw the headline in the daily paper. "Board Nixes Belts," followed by "Are our kids at risk?" and a long article in which the parent group was quoted extensively: "We were told that school buses were safer without seat belts. What about those kids who were killed in California then?" And, "We need a more responsive school board," and, "We need a business manager more concerned about kids than dollars."

The Dilemma

That afternoon Mr. Doyle was called into the superintendent's office. The superintendent had not been quoted in the paper, and Mr. Doyle recalled that he had not commented on the seat belt issue during last night's school board meeting. "What I want you to do," he said, "is update the figures on the seat belt thing. Bring in all the factors that might cause expenses to go clear through the roof. Find out the dope on seat belt failure and misuse. Concentrate on the negative stuff."

As Mr. Doyle began to assemble his information, he found that costs were definitely greater. But he also received other data, alarming data, on school bus brake failures, side impact crashes, students leaving their seats during travel, bus driver negligence, and maintenance issues. Further, there was more traffic locally than there had been six years ago, since a new highway was built that was used by the buses. The more he learned, the more Mr. Doyle became convinced that the proper use of seat belts in school buses could indeed save children from injuries and worse.

When he wrote the draft of the report, he documented the higher costs but also included the new information on injury-causing situations. The following day, the business manager met with the superintendent to report his findings. The superintendent was not pleased. "What I want you to do," he said, "is just emphasize the high expenses. We run a good transportation program here and I don't think that this other stuff is relevant. When you get your report finished, we'll send it to the school board and let them handle the fallout."

The Decision Point

Mr. Doyle now faced a dilemma. If he included the positive information about seat belts in the report, it could show that, despite the expense, seat belts might be justified. If Mr. Doyle suppressed these data, however, he might be leaving out a crucial body of information relative to school bus safety and the welfare of children.

Analysis of the Case

This is a case that can easily be viewed through multiple frameworks. From a justice perspective, it seems clear that the SBO is working within the letter of the law. If he considers the greater good for the greater number, in times of limited resources, it may seem more prudent to attend to the needs of all students, not just bus students, by expending resources to raise test scores. After all, the federal law, No Child Left Behind, binds school officials in this way. On the other hand, the SBO needs to recognize that students and their parents have rights, and schools have a moral obligation to keep students safe.

A caring perspective would likely view this situation as nonnurturing, a hierarchical decision that ignores personal connections. Certainly an important part of caring is promoting the welfare and physical safety of students. Here the SBO would need to consider whether keeping the new information about the effectiveness of seat belts in preventing injuries and fatalities secret is the caring thing to do and if such actions weaken the school climate or endanger the students.

Viewing this dilemma from a power perspective, the SBO might question the justice of an old policy (no seat belts on buses) in light of new information that, if known, might provide a basis for changing the policy. He might also question who made the old policy and who is enforcing the current school policy. Does the SBO or the superintendent care about the safety of the children in this school district or do they simply want to maintain the status quo? Knowledge is power. Should the

SBO follow the superintendent's instructions to leave out new information favoring seat belts? Is the superintendent abusing his authority for financial or other reasons? Viewed from this perspective, the SBO's withholding of valuable information could well be an abuse of power.

In this case, the community could be the school board members who might not be reelected if they'd have to raise taxes to pay for seat belts. It could also include older citizens on fixed incomes, who might have to pay more at greater personal sacrifice to enforce a policy that is not required by law or proven by statistics. The community is also represented by parents who genuinely fear for their children's safety and by school board members who support this view. Here, the SBO needs to reflect on his commitment to the community and whether withholding or providing the new information is part of this commitment.

Considering the professional framework, the SBO would have to decide whether taking additional, perhaps unnecessary measures to keep bus students safe is more in the best interests of students than raising test scores, which could well determine their academic futures and career choices. One might also look to the ASBO standards of conduct, which require SBOs to "interpret the policies and practices of the district . . . to the community fairly and objectively" and to "assist fellow administrators as appropriate in fulfilling their obligations."

Outcome

Mr. Doyle got busy. He checked to see what other districts had done with the seat belt issue. He talked with business managers and transportation directors. He stated his case and asked for feedback. He was told, "Don't rock the boat," and "Listen to your conscience," and "It will blow over," and "We put in seat belts and it's working," and "We put in seat belts and it didn't work." He also got a lot of suggestions for implementation.

In all good conscience, he could not recommend against the use of seat belts. However, he decided on a compromise to take to the superintendent. In his report, he cautiously stated the fact that injuries could occur, but that seat belts were only one way to prevent them. He came up with a plan to phase in belts, starting with one or more buses for elementary school children, and adding belts each year to "see how it worked." He suggested that the routes using the new highway have priority for belts. An evaluation would then be done after each year, including a parent survey, to garner information about the new safety measures.

At the school board meeting, Mr. Doyle found his report, unaltered, quite acceptable to the board, as well as the parent group, with the superintendent taking all the credit.

FROM THEORY TO PRACTICE

Perhaps now more than ever, school business officials must be keenly aware of their own ethical values and the various approaches to ethical decision making. This chapter has provided an example of an analytical process using five different theoretical frameworks to help solve an ethical dilemma. Knowledge of these frameworks, coupled with development of their own personal and professional codes of ethics and an awareness of the ASBO code of conduct, will assist SBOs in resolving ethical dilemmas that occur in their professional life. Part II of this book provides a series of other ethical dilemmas for readers to analyze and reflect on in order to improve the ethical decisions they must make in their day-to-day work.

Part II

APPLYING ETHICAL PERSPECTIVES

Part II concentrates on applying the concepts described in part I to ethical dilemmas similar to the ones school business officials frequently encounter. These dilemmas were written primarily by practicing SBOs. Rather than attempt to cover every aspect of the SBO's job, the authors of this book decided to include dilemmas that are representative of issues that SBOs face most often.

Most of the dilemmas fall under three of the seven broad categories presented in the ASBO professional standards: human resource management, financial resource management, and ancillary services. Three other categories were combined because there were fewer representative cases in these areas: facility management, property acquisition and management, and information management. The reader should keep in mind, however, that these categories are used to help organize the cases according to their primary focus. As in real life, these dilemmas present complex, multifaceted problems that easily cross categorical lines.

Likewise, the ASBO standard addressing the educational enterprise is not specifically mentioned because its major elements—organization, administration, public policy, intergovernmental relations, and legal issues—are present to some extent in all the cases. Indeed, all the cases heavily emphasize legal issues because of the strong possibility of grave consequences and also because law and ambiguities surrounding the law figure into so many ethical dilemmas that SBOs encounter.

For easy reading, the cases are organized into a consistent format. First, there is background information. Second is a description of the dilemma. A decision point for the SBO is next. Questions for discussion follow. All in all, there are fourteen cases emphasizing a multitude of issues of vital importance to SBOs. The case outcomes are described in a separate chapter at the end of the book.

6

HUMAN RESOURCE MANAGEMENT

As articulated in the ASBO standards, dealing within a human context is central to the SBO's work. Here the focus is on serving effectively as part of an executive team within the school district. Human resource management functions include issues related to personnel and benefits administration, professional development, labor relations and employment agreements, and human relations. The cases below represent broad aspects of these areas. They focus on retirement benefits, conflicts of interest, and negotiations. Ethical issues as well as loyalty concerns are key to resolving the problems these dilemmas present.

CASE 1: RETIREMENT BENEFITS AGREEMENT: UNDERSTANDING THE BIG PICTURE

It was no secret that Rod Wilson, the superintendent of the White Oak School District, was going to retire at the end of the school year after twenty-five years of service to the district. He had served ten years as the assistant superintendent and the past fifteen years as the superintendent.

Mr. Wilson was admired by the community and staff and the district had made great educational strides during his tenure. The board was beginning the search process for a new superintendent and dealing with the normal transition issues that accompany such a change. Part of that transition was reviewing, clarifying, and granting the current retiring superintendent some benefits for postretirement.

Marge Stewart, the business manager in the White Oak District, was fairly well established and had been with the district for the past eight years. Prior to that, she had performed various school business official duties at two other districts and was within a year or two of retirement as well. The relationship between the business manager and superintendent had always been both cordial and professional. One expectation the superintendent maintained, however, was that no one talked to the district solicitor except the superintendent.

In April, Mr. Wilson and Mrs. Stewart were meeting to finalize some budget issues for the next year when the superintendent jokingly commented about making sure there was enough in the budget to pay his bonus and free hospitalization coverage as granted by the board.

"Oh yeah, and maybe we should add a new budget line for my health benefits—just so you all don't forget about me," he chuckled.

The business manager was somewhat taken by surprise, "What do you mean? Are you serious or just pulling my leg?"

"Well, actually, yes, I am quite serious," the superintendent replied. "You see, in December, a board action took place and granted certain benefits, including the free hospitalization coverage for me and my wife as part of my total retirement package."

Marge started to explain that there could be some difficulty implementing that benefit under the current structure of the district's health insurance plan. The superintendent immediately cut her off. "The deal is set. You just make sure it happens," he ordered her.

With that, Mr. Wilson ended the session and left the room. Marge knew that, based on past practice with other administrators, there would be some kind of severance pay to the superintendent, especially one with such a long and distinguished service record. However, the free hospitalization coverage was news to her at this point, as well as the part about its being approved several months ago.

The Dilemma

As the business manager mulled this over, she realized that there were several items she or the board would have to deal with. The business manager attended all school board meetings. She had been at the meeting last December and knew that the agreement described by the superintendent had not been made in public. Additionally, and of more concern, the district was self-insured for hospitalization and the plan for coverage eligibility was very specific about such requirements.

Mrs. Stewart had worked in another district previously and was aware of IRS and legal differences between premium-based insurance plans and self-insurance. Their self-insurance plan clearly stipulated that retirement coverage was provided for retirees who met the stated district or state eligibility criteria and that the retirees paid for the coverage. In researching the dilemma further, she discovered through a phone conversation to the district reinsurance carrier that "the district can 'insure' anyone it wants; however, if you cover someone 'outside' of the plan, document eligibility rules state that you are on your own."

In essence, this meant that any claim above the district's specific reinsurance cap of $100,000 would be borne by district funds and not the insurer. Any large claim exposure would be a district liability. The superintendent's spouse was having medical problems. Mr. Wilson was fifty-five years old and would likely be on the district plan until age sixty-five. The chances of a large claim from either one of these two individuals over the period of the next ten years was probably higher than normal given that the superintendent also had some ongoing medical issues.

To complicate matters further, a benefits lawyer informed the business manager that providing such a benefit is discriminatory when involving highly compensated individuals and could have serious consequences for the district. The same lawyer suggested that the district should consult with a tax professional. If the benefit was indeed discriminatory, there would be tax liability for both the district and the superintendent. The lawyer jokingly said, "One solution would be to grant free coverage to every retiree and there would be no discrimination issue. Your taxpayers may have a thing or two to say about that!" The business manager's research had validated her initial concerns and now it was time to make some decisions.

The Decision Point

Mrs. Stewart had always gotten along well with the superintendent and was highly respected by the board. Both relationships seemed at risk over this issue. To implement this "agreement," the district would be assuming a large financial risk and, most definitely, there were some legal and tax ramifications. If the business manager did nothing, there was a reasonable chance that none of these issues would ever surface. After all, she was planning to retire in two years and free hospitalization didn't sound like too bad of a deal. To stir things up with the board, not knowing exactly what they understood about these issues, could complicate working relationships and blemish the last impressions of otherwise distinguished careers. And certainly the issue could taint the business manager's working relationship with any new superintendent and board.

Mrs. Stewart was not even sure if there was a recorded agreement that could be referenced for payment authority. She also knew that the superintendent was pretty astute when it came to hospitalization issues, so there was a great deal of uncertainty about how much disclosure was actually made to the board, whether the solicitor had been involved, or if such omission was due to lack of knowledge and research. On the other hand, if something happened to open this benefit up to inspection while the business manager was still there, things could get really nasty!

Questions for Discussion

1. From a legal perspective, a contract is valid only if both parties agree. If one party reconsiders, based on hidden information that changes the agreement, then the contract would likely be invalidated. Does the agreement between the superintendent and the school board constitute a valid contract? If the board or the superintendent can legally change the contract, should they? From a legal standpoint, does it matter that the negotiations were not made public? From an ethical perspective, does it matter that the negotiations were not made public?

2. From a justice perspective, is the agreement a fair one? To the superintendent? To the district? Considering the potential financial

hardship for the district, how might one analyze this situation from the perspective of "the greater good for the greater number"? Equal respect for the individual's rights?

3. How might one view this dilemma from a caring perspective? Who should be the object of care here? The superintendent who has devoted his career to the school district? The superintendent's sick wife? The teachers, parents, and students in the district? Anyone else?

4. From a critical perspective, who has the power here? Why do you think the SBO was not made aware of the agreement? Is the superintendent abusing his power? Does it matter that he is well liked? Has served the district well for a number of years? Has a sick wife? Kept the agreement secret? Is the school board abusing its power? Who is the school board representing in this case?

5. From a professional perspective, is this agreement in the best interests of the students? Could there be clashes between the SBO's personal and professional codes of ethics? Does the SBO owe a duty of loyalty to the superintendent? To the school board? How far does this duty extend?

6. Is there an obligation to the community? If not, why not? If there is, what is it?

7. What would you do if you were Marge Stewart? Explain the rationale for your decision from an ethical perspective.

CASE 2: TARNISHED SILVER

Two adjacent suburban school districts, Silverdale and Plainville, have always presented a contrast. Silverdale, encompassing a number of large, expensive, upscale housing developments, is rich, while Plainville, closer to the central urban area, is much poorer.

As business manager for Plainville, John was well aware of his district's fiscal shortcomings. His sister Mary was a secretary in the Silverdale district office, and from time to time at family gatherings, John heard about Silverdale's well-heeled situation—their building program, sports facilities, new equipment, and the like. Was he envious? Probably, he admitted to himself. Mary kidded him about his district's need to count pennies, but it was good-natured, and he kidded her back about their being poor but honest.

Mary and her husband had lived in Silverdale for a long time, and since she used her husband's last name, her relation to John was not generally known. A friendly, outgoing person, Mary was popular with her coworkers. Connie, the new business manager hired by the Silverdale district, especially liked Mary. Connie would stop by Mary's desk and chat, often join her for lunch. She and Mary would engage in what could best be described as "girl talk," with Connie doing most of the talking. Connie was single and liked to talk about her boyfriends and Mary found her fascinating.

During the ensuing year, Silverdale decided to buy new computers, purchasing new models with the latest software. In addition, training for teachers in the new equipment was envisioned. All this was going to involve considerable expense, and representatives from the major computer companies began visiting the district to discuss their products.

The Dilemma

At about this time, Connie started telling Mary about a new boyfriend, Doug. She had met him when he came to the district office, representing one of the computer companies that would be bidding on the contract. As the weeks went by, Mary heard about how wonderful Doug was, how generous, how serious he was about her; it was clear that Connie was well into an affair. Soon Connie began confiding all sorts of intimate details of their relationship. Mary did not know how to tell Connie that she did not want to hear all of this, but she did know it was told in confidence and should not be repeated. Connie looked radiant and happy, and Mary let her talk on.

"I really want to help Doug get ahead," she told Mary one day. "It's clear he has great potential in the computer business, and when he lands this Silverdale contract, it is bound to lead to a promotion, a raise, and who knows what for our future together!"

"But there's a lot of competition," Mary said, "and it's a complicated process, getting just what the district wants."

"Don't worry! I have it all figured out!" exclaimed Connie. She tapped her finger against her forehead. "I'm the one responsible for developing the specifications, and all I have to do is write them so that Doug's product is the perfect fit!" Connie beamed.

The Decision Point

In one month the school board would meet to award the computer contract. Mary needed to talk to someone about Connie's confession. She decided to go to her big brother. Mary was not happy with the relationship that had developed between Connie and herself, but she had gotten herself into it and was going to clear the air. She spared no details.

John heard her out and was appalled. He realized that Connie was running for board of directors of the state ASBO. He couldn't believe that a fellow business manager would consider something so blatantly illegal or unethical. But now that he knew, what could he do? How could he tarnish another business manager's reputation? Then he was simply disgusted that she was engaging in an affair with someone trying to gain benefits from the district. People connected with public education were held to a pretty high standard. Further, he was mad at Connie for making Mary an accessory by confiding in her. It was a tricky situation, and his little sister was involved.

"John, I'm sorry to have dumped this all on you!" wailed Mary. "I didn't know who else I could tell; I can't lose my job!"

"It's all right," said John. "We'll get it worked out."

Questions for Discussion

1. What are the legal implications of Connie's contemplated actions if she carries them out? What are the legal implications for Mary if she goes along with Connie? What are the legal implications for John if he remains silent? Does John have a legal responsibility to report Connie?
2. If designing contracts to meet specifications of outside vendors was a common practice at Silverdale and no one seemed to think it was wrong, should that influence John's decision? Why or why not?
3. From an ethical perspective, what would be the fair thing for John to do? Is it fair for John to report Connie, considering that Mary revealed the information to him in confidence?

4. Mary is John's sister. Does John have a higher duty to protect family than to reveal illegal wrongdoing? If John remains silent and no one finds out that John has this information, does that make a difference? What would a caring person do, given John's dilemma?

5. If Connie designs the specifications to match Doug's product, is this an abuse of power? Why or why not? If Doug's product really would help the school district, would your answer to the first question change? Why or why not?

6. If John were basing his actions on the expectations of the profession, what course of action should he take? Why? What decision would be in the best interests of the students at Silverdale? Because John does not work at Silverdale, would he still have a professional obligation to look out for the best interests of their students?

7. Does Mary, Connie, or John have a duty to the community? If so, what is it?

8. What would you do if you were John? Explain the rationale for your decision from an ethical perspective.

CASE 3: THE BLACK ROCK SCHOOL DISTRICT NEGOTIATIONS IMPASSE

The Black Rock School District was in the eleventh month of teacher negotiations with the 352-member bargaining unit. Negotiations had gotten off to a bad start and continued to deteriorate over the course of nearly a year. The district and teachers were in their fourth month of the new school year without a contract. Fortunately everyone seemed to be operating (under the status quo) well enough to keep the schools open and kids learning. At least they were until the last teachers association meeting. Now a strike seemed to be imminent and the teachers united in their resolve.

The school board and its negotiating team were frustrated. From their view, the usual main issues of money, benefits, and time seemed to have been reasonably worked out. However, the teachers were insisting on major language changes for just cause, employment rights, and working conditions. The new language changes were seen as severely restricting managerial rights and simply were not acceptable to the board, or even the new superintendent. The board thought these items would disappear as "economic" issues were handled. That assumption now looked like a severe miscalculation, with animosity across the bargaining table running at an all-time high.

Nearly two years before while working on an early-bird settlement, the prior superintendent had had a rather nasty personnel case thrust on him. The result was a very public dismissal of Mr. Rankin, a long-term, well-liked teacher. This particular case shut down the early-bird negotiations and remained the underlying cause of many of the strong labor feelings and resentment the two sides were now dealing with. Since that time, a new superintendent had been hired and three new board members elected. The professional staff relationship with the new administration had gone extremely well, with many positive things happening in the schools. So while the teachers seemed pleased with the changes and direction of a new administration, they remained adamant about their current demands.

Mr. James, the business manager for Black Rock, had been involved, along with the former superintendent, with the personnel case that had created this apparent rallying point. In fact, Mr. James was the only remaining district staff member who had any firsthand knowledge of the facts of the prior situation. Mr. James was proud of the way he and the former superintendent had handled that sensitive and volatile case. But it had been clear from the very beginning that a large volume of misinformation was now circulating in the community regarding the case. Mr. James was fairly certain that the former staff member was probably contributing to those issues for personal reasons. Two of the prior board members (the personnel committee) had been briefed after the case was resolved, but the rest of the board, potentially serving as the hearing panel, was not prejudiced with details of the incident.

The Dilemma

Cliff Rankin, the teacher in question, had worked for the district thirty-two years and was, by all accounts, a well-liked, respected member of the district and local community. He had begun his career at the district's middle school and ten years ago had accepted a transfer to a high school position. Enrollment and curriculum changes created a need and fit for Cliff to return to the middle school to teach in a newly updated curriculum program. At first he resisted the transfer but then consented, but not before lodging a formal complaint with the union for a potential grievance. The transfer information was discussed at a public board meeting and was reported in the local press, along with all other agenda items.

Two days after this transfer, while the superintendent was out, Mr. James received a phone call from a concerned middle school parent who said she would *not* allow her daughter to attend any classes with Mr. Rankin. After several minutes on the phone, Mr. James knew they had a serious problem. It took several requests by Mr. James to have the parent leave her name and phone number. He had to promise her that no names would be revealed at this point nor would they be at a later date without her permission. Mr. James affirmed that if there were any accusations made, and if there were any truth to them, appropriate action would be taken. He immediately got in touch with the superintendent and they then set up a meeting with the parent.

From Mr. James's perspective, the superintendent did a terrific job during the meeting with an obviously distraught, yet sincere parent. In a nutshell, the parent disclosed that Mr. Rankin had been physically inappropriate with her years before when she had been a student of his. With her own daughter now in middle school, it was just too much for her to bear and she was determined that her daughter was not going to sit in his class. More alarmingly, she claimed to know three other parents in the community who had the same experiences with this teacher when they were students; they would also come forward if something were not done.

The parent was extremely upset and clearly did not want this issue to become public due to the impact on her and her family. Unfortunately other innocent community members, as well as Mr. Rankin's family, would be involved. Mr. James and the superintendent spent the next hour reviewing all options and speaking with the district solicitor. The superintendent then made up his mind.

Cliff Rankin thought he was being called to the superintendent's office regarding the transfer issue and told several peers in the teacher's lounge as much. When arriving at the superintendent's office, he was informed that Mr. James would be in attendance. The superintendent got right to the point and presented the charges. Cliff, visibly stunned, broke down immediately and admitted he was indeed guilty of some indiscretions. Emotionally, he explained that all of this was in his past and he had, for several years, been involved in programs to help with his "problem," including treatment and therapy. Cliff pleaded, "All the incidents happened over twenty years ago, and there have been absolutely no problems since!"

The superintendent very clearly and directly informed Mr. Rankin that he had until the end of the day to resign or he would take the next appropriate step to dismiss him formally. "I have the sole authority," he explained, trying to remain calm, "under the state education code and the Child Protection Act to dismiss you right this moment and have you escorted off the campus." Additionally, the superintendent told Cliff that Mr. James would immediately process a purchase of service for his military time, which would allow for a full retirement option. He would be placed on paid leave until all paperwork was finalized. It was made clear these were his only options.

In the meantime, Mr. Rankin would not be allowed in the district buildings. The superintendent said that if Cliff resigned right here and now, the superintendent would do his best to protect the privacy of all involved. It would end right here. All parties would agree to confidentiality. The superintendent also said that he would not seek to have Mr. Rankin's teaching certificate revoked, unless Cliff sought employment at another district where he would be required to provide a reference, which the superintendent would not do. Mr. Rankin agreed on the spot, signed a prepared resignation, and left the office.

Relieved, upset, and confused all at the same time, Mr. James inquired into the superintendent's actions: "Why did you allow him such guaranteed confidentiality?"

"Because I promised the child's mother, and through her, the other women involved. This is a small community and I don't want those families to be punished for *his* actions just because we think there should be a witch hunt. Believe me, don't you think I wanted to string him up?" the superintendent explained.

"I see," Mr. James's voice faded, but he still wondered if the decision to not revoke the license unless Mr. Rankin pursued another teaching job was the right one.

Not surprisingly, within the hour, the superintendent's phone was ringing off the hook as word spread that he had summarily fired this long-term district veteran employee. There were a lot of angry people. The other teachers had immediately pressed Cliff to file a lawsuit and grievance against the district. They were convinced that Mr. Rankin resigned due to conflicts related to his grievance about the transfer. Cliff wanted no part of a lawsuit and said so, but the union threatened to take the case forward without him.

Misinformation abounded and the teachers rallied around Cliff. Once it was clear that Cliff did not want to challenge the district, they focused their energies on the labor language issues they believed would protect union members in the future. The cry was heard, "If the district could do this to a thirty-plus-year employee, what about those with less service?" The superintendent, in the final year of his contract and slated for retirement himself, took an inordinate amount of public and staff pressure over the issue. But he remained true to his word to the parents, and the real reason for Cliff's leaving the district was never made public.

The Decision Point

Now a critical negotiation session was scheduled for the following evening. The day before this session, representatives of the two sides were to meet informally without their full teams to see if anything could be done to move the negotiations forward. Mr. James was convinced that the underlying misinformation about the Cliff Rankin case was what stood in Black Rock's way, not only for these negotiations but for future ongoing labor relations. He had kept his silence out of respect for the former superintendent's handling of the case and the people involved. However, he never anticipated the district's "paying" in such a disruptive and long-term manner for what he saw as a good deed.

Representing the district was the new superintendent, Dr. Janice Davis, Mr. James, and the board's lead negotiator. Representing the union was their Uniserve representative, along with their president and one other officer. The union's president was an influential leader. The union's Uniserve representative was in his first negotiation with this bargaining unit and did not possess much clout. The other union officer, in Mr. James's view, was a busybody whose ability to maintain confidentiality was questionable.

Mr. James felt frustrated since he was the only member of either side who knew what really happened. His thought was that if several other key people on the negotiating teams understood the issues involved in that case, there might be a chance to reach compromise and reestablish and rebuild trust between the two sides. He was torn with the belief that if he were to trust members of the union and members of his own team with such information, there would be no guarantee that people would not talk. Breaking that trust would have implications for many lives in the community. As time for the informal meeting approached, Mr. James had to make his decision.

Questions for Discussion

1. What legal issues are involved in this case? Did the former superintendent violate the law in the way he handled this case? Why or why not?
2. Was the handling of the previous situation fair to Mr. Rankin? Mr. Rankin's family? The parent who wished to remain anonymous? The other parents with children in the school? Mr. James? The current teachers and union representatives? Dr. Davis, the new superintendent? What would be the fairest way to resolve the current situation with the teachers and their union?
3. What would be the most caring way to resolve the current situation?
4. Does either the former or current dilemma involve an abuse of power? Why or why not?
5. How would the profession expect Mr. James to resolve the negotiations impasse?
6. What actions on Mr. James's part would be in the best interests of the students? The community?
7. What would you do if you were Mr. James? Explain the rationale for your decision from an ethical perspective.

CASE 4: TRAVEL EXPENSES FOR SPECIAL EDUCATION

To serve its speech impaired and learning disabled students, a mostly rural school district, Far Horizons, had to rely heavily on itinerant teachers serving a number of widely separated schools. For years associated expenses such as mileage were fairly consistent, with an occasional overnight motel and meal expense when winter storms warranted caution.

The Dilemma

During a mild winter, one itinerant special education teacher, Jim, began regularly submitting expenses for overnight stays and meals. The business manager, Jane, having questions about payment for his expenses, decided to get together with Beth, his supervisor. Beth took the opportunity to express her concerns about Jim.

"He's been with us for ten years. I don't understand it," said Beth. "I've also noted that he requests more materials than my other teachers although he is actually working with fewer students."

Jane asked Beth to see if she could learn more about the situation by talking to Jim. "Oh, I have," replied Beth, "and he says he is sometimes so tired by the end of his day that it would be hazardous to drive home. You know, he was recently divorced and it left him very down, although lately he seems better. He's really popular with all the teachers. Everyone likes him; you can't help it. He has such a nice way about him. Maybe you could talk to him."

Jane agreed. She also decided to get more information on the problem first. The expense reports Jim turned in indicated that his overnight stays were all in one part of the county. Since she had planned to visit some outlying district schools on another matter, Jane added that area to her list and made sure to go on a day when Jim was not scheduled to be there.

When Jane met with the principal of the elementary school Jim served, she learned that Jim worked with six learning disabled students during his time on-site. The principal enthusiastically declared that Jim did an outstanding job and added, "It's exhausting work sometimes, with these kids."

At the middle school, Jane found out that Jim saw a group of eight to ten speech impaired students. Again, the assistant principal praised Jim and his hard work. Jane was ready to leave when a student who had been nearby said, "And he always goes out to Mrs. Jensen's farm to help her disabled son. I know he spends a lot of time there because I've seen his car parked in the driveway at night when we go to choir practice."

Jane asked, "Is Mrs. Jensen's son in your class too?"

"Oh, no," replied the student. "He's twenty-three."

The Decision Point

A few days later, Jane called Jim's supervisor to her office to tell her what she'd learned. While she confirmed Beth's observation of his being a good teacher, as well as providing a reason for his using more materials, Jane expressed her skepticism about the reason for Jim's overnight stays.

But instead of being appreciative of Jane's information, Beth was upset. "I don't think it was right for you to snoop around and check up on Jim like that! He is one of our best teachers and I'm sure he's only trying to help someone who has slipped through the cracks."

"Good intentions or not," Jane told her, "I don't feel I can authorize payment for these expenses."

At that, Beth left in a huff. Sometime later, Jane took the next step and arranged a meeting with Jim and Beth. The following week, when the meeting time arrived, Jane looked up to see Beth holding the door open for Jim, who hobbled in on crutches. He grinned sheepishly.

"Almost fell asleep on the drive home last Friday," he said. "Fortunately, only twisted my ankle in the panic to get the car back on the road."

Jane sighed. The dilemma of Jim's expense requests was not going to be easy to solve.

Questions for Discussion

1. Are there legal issues is this case? If so, what are they?
2. Considering this situation, what is the fair course of action?
3. Is there an issue of caring in this situation? If so, who needs to be considered in this respect? How would you handle it?

4. Who has the power in this situation? Is power being used appropriately?
5. Does the community have a stake in the outcome of this case? If so, how? If not, why not?
6. What would the profession expect of Jane in this situation?
7. What actions are in the best interests of the students?
8. What would you do if you were Jane? Explain the rationale for your decision from an ethical perspective.

7

FINANCIAL RESOURCE MANAGEMENT

It goes without saying that financial resource management is critical to the SBO's everyday work responsibilities. The ASBO professional standards state explicitly that SBOs need to understand basic financial principles associated with "school finance, budgeting, financial planning, accounting, auditing, financial reporting, cash management, investments, debt management, and technology for school business operations" (ASBO 2001, 11). Not only must professionals comprehend these principles, they must also demonstrate their knowledge through practical application.

Applying such principles, however, is not always as straightforward as it sounds. Some issues may be clearly right or wrong, as in the case of illegal business transactions. But in other situations there are no clear-cut rules. SBOs may encounter serious ethical issues involving personnel, vendors, and others affiliated with the district, such as parent groups. The dilemmas in this chapter illustrate complex situations focusing on how money is spent for items such as travel, consultants, and sports equipment, as well as oversight responsibility for school-related money held by other groups.

CASE 5: USE OF CONSULTANTS

"Hey, it's good to see you guys. I've thought about you since I left that last position I had a couple of years ago, where we saw each other more often. It's always great to get together with people you haven't seen and catch up. Maybe that's the best part of the state conference. Anyhow, now that you're here, I wonder if I could tell you about what's been happening in my district. I'm in a dilemma, and maybe you guys could help me out.

"When I took this new job as business manager for the district, it seemed to be an ideal situation. My friends said, 'Bob, you've got it made.' A good-size district, fairly wealthy, with a great school board that had every confidence in the superintendent, things went very well that first year. And the super himself was a really dedicated and innovative professional. He got his Ph.D. from one of the best graduate schools of education in the country, and the prestige hung around him—I'd say well deserved— like an aura. His connections were impressive and several professors from his alma mater came down to our district to serve as consultants, presenting to the school board, doing studies, that sort of thing. They were, of course, well paid. I know, because I authorized payment for their fees. But we were certainly very close to the top district in the state, student-achievement-wise."

The Dilemma

"Well, you know it couldn't last. Our super was asked to take over a senior position in the U.S. Department of Education—very important. How could he refuse such a great honor? So off he went to Washington, D.C. Before he left, he had more or less hand-picked his successor. Who would question his judgment? Not me. The new super, I'll call him Dr. Jones, was maybe not as well-known or as well-respected in the field. How could he be? But we were all glad to support him as he tried to fill the shoes of his distinguished predecessor.

"Now, I'm not one to complain or to question my superior's policies, but over the year I began to notice more and more requests for payments to consultants being submitted—expenses, honorariums, and so on. My job was to approve the expenditures and nothing else, so I continued to do so. But consultants' fees were getting pretty high, much higher than they used to be. And there were an awful lot of consultants, but none of the ones we used to get from the university and all."

The Decision Point

"At the school board meetings I found myself listening for mention of the fact that a Mr. So-and-So from some consulting firm was going to come down to help out with Such-and-Such, or a Ms. Someone-or-Other from an educational associates group was going to do a study here linking Something-with-Something. It used to be that way under our old super—keeping the school board up with what was going on in the way of consultants. Month after month, no mention of studies or consultants was made in the meetings, and month after month, I did the authorization to pay Mr. So-and-So and Ms. Someone-or-Other for professional educational services to the district.

"What I did hear in the school board meetings was that with the new mandates and the charter school movement, the district was going to have to hold the line on expenses. The board came up with certain targets for reduced spending—no new hires and limiting out-of-state travel: I remember thinking, 'Darn! There goes my trip to ASBO!' The third point was to severely curtail the use of consultants.

"So you see, I was beginning to wonder about all this. I'm thinking that the school board doesn't know what's going on, consultant-wise. I'm thinking maybe I ought to talk to someone. Just to make sure I'm not on the wrong track. Not that I doubt Dr. Jones's judgment, of course. I mean, there was this precedent for consultants, after all. So I'm glad to see you guys. What do you think?"

Questions for Discussion

1. Are there possible legal issues involved in this dilemma? If so, what are they?
2. Is Bob dealing with any fairness issues? If so, what are they and how should he handle them?
3. Does Bob owe a duty of care to Dr. Jones? What is his responsibility with respect to the school board? The community?

4. How did the former superintendent use his power with respect to consultants? How is Dr. Jones using his power in this regard? Did either or both abuse their power? If so, how? Compare and contrast the two methods of handling the use of consultants.
5. What would the profession expect Bob to do in this situation? How should Bob handle this situation with the school board? The community?
6. What action would be in the best interests of the students?
7. What would you do if you were Bob? Explain the rationale for your decision from an ethical perspective.

CASE 6: PURCHASING FOOTBALL EQUIPMENT

It was early July and a few items were still needed for the fall sports season that was set to begin in five weeks. The athletic director, Fred Simpson, was responsible for placing orders for the athletic teams, after the orders were reviewed and approved by the district purchasing agent. The coaching staff provided him with the details on what equipment and supplies were needed and specific brands and vendors. (Both the athletic director and veteran coaches had developed relationships with salespeople who regularly provided information on the latest, greatest equipment on the market.)

While inventorying the football equipment for the next season, an assistant coach discovered a batch of helmets that had been ruined in a spring flood in one of the storage units. The helmets' safety features had been compromised and there was no way to rely on them with confidence if they were used. The athletic director immediately contacted a salesman he had dealt with frequently in the past to see if his company could supply the needed helmets.

The company had them, but they would have to be ordered ASAP—it would take four weeks to get the order processed and the helmets emblazoned with the school logo. So he went ahead and sent a requisition to the purchasing agent to buy the helmets from Sports Warehouse at a cost of $5,123. He also jotted on the purchase order that he realized he was "beyond his budget," but that the Booster Club was willing to pick up the remaining balance. He and the Boosters had agreed that all of the helmets should be replaced, since the team would look rather silly with mismatched helmets and there had already been a discussion about looking into a new style of helmet for the entire team.

State law required securing three quotes for orders of similar items exceeding $4,000. This requirement was intended to relieve some of the burden of formal bidding but still promote competition in pricing. The quotes could be verbal quotes and were not as formal as the bidding process. After receiving the requisition, the purchasing agent notified the athletic director that price quotes from two other companies were needed before the order could be placed.

The Dilemma

The athletic director immediately went to the business office to demand answers from the purchasing agent, Tom Wilkes. "Tom, what is this all about? We've gone the route of bidding before and it didn't work. Time is critical here. Why are you insisting we follow this stupid procedure? I have better things to do than spend time gathering quotes because of a stupid requirement. We need those helmets and we need them now. We can't practice or play any games until we have them. The Boosters are not going to be happy with this delay when I have to report tonight at their meeting. Oh, and by the way, Sports Warehouse has the exact helmet we want," Fred exclaimed.

"Sorry, Fred, but I don't make the rules. I still need those quotes. Every year the district records are audited and one of the things they look for is whether we adhere to the purchasing guidelines. The district received audit citations a few years ago, before I came here, because of its purchasing practices. The superintendent and business manager made it clear to me when I was hired that the process must be cleaned up," insisted the purchasing agent.

"So! Follow it most of the time. What are the chances they'll find this one? You know, Tom, Sports Warehouse has been very good to us. We've had a long-standing relationship with them that I won't jeopardize. They've gotten us into their coaches clinic even when we forgot to send in our registrations, and they've even picked up the tab for two of our coaches to attend for the past several years. They've treated us well! Why can't you just overlook this? Better yet, Tom, why don't you just split the order in half and put it on two purchase orders? That way neither one will be over the limit and you can spare me all of this hassle."

"Fred, we seem to have this conversation periodically. We are not allowed to split orders like that just to avoid the bidding threshold. I need the quotes. The sooner you get them to me, the sooner I can take care of your order and the sooner we'll get the helmets."

Two days later the purchase request appeared on Tom's desk again for review. Attached to it was a summary of the two additional quotes the athletic director secured. The price from Sports Warehouse was the lowest of the three quotes and, in fact, it was lower than the original price. The purchase order was prepared for Sports Warehouse and faxed to them.

A week later, Tom received a call from Football Specialists asking for the results of the quotes. The salesman made a comment that gave him the impression that the quotes were not secured in an unbiased fashion. He indicated he had helmets in stock and could have shipped them in three weeks. He told Tom that the athletic director indicated his quote was lower than the others, but said one of the other companies offered some perks and he preferred to do business with them. He warned Tom that if the district continues with these practices, he might be forced to look into legal action.

Tom visited with Fred again and asked him to describe the process by which the quotes were secured. Fred responded that he secured quotes from the two other companies and when one was lower than Sports Warehouse's, he called the Sports Warehouse salesman and shared the other quotes he received. In turn, Sports Warehouse dropped its price to match the low quote and offered to have the helmets emblazoned with the district's logo as required in the specifications *and* add "2000–2001–2003 State Champions." As a way of saying thanks for the business, he included a couple of tickets for Fred to a nearby professional baseball game.

"So," Fred gloated, "everything is hunky-dory, right? You got your three quotes *and* the lowest bid is now lower than before. I got to save the district's good relationship with Sports Warehouse, and we are getting great equipment *in time* for the season! We're both winners, wouldn't you say?"

The Decision Point

Tom took this new information to the business manager, Al Brookes, and suggested that they cancel the purchase order to Sports Warehouse and get the quotes again on a fair basis. They reviewed the events to date, including the perks Sports Warehouse provided (both the ones they knew about and the possibility there were other perks they didn't know about), and they discussed the ramifications of clashing with the team that had brought pride back to the community with their state football championships. They considered the time crunch they were in and the fact that the Booster Club had a couple of school board members among its membership. The business manager also thought about his contract, which was up for renewal in two months, and how this would be the kind of thing that could easily throw a snag in it.

"What do you think, Al?" inquired Tom.

"Well, we do have some legal ramifications here. You say that another vendor called you personally to complain about the bidding process?" asked Al.

"That's right."

"*And* they know about the special things that coaches often get from this Sports Warehouse?" Al returned.

"How do you think I found out? Heck, they told me! Other than the things Fred had already told me. But he made it out to sound as if the company is a pillar of the community!" Tom exclaimed.

"Well, now, they may be. I have already gotten a memo from the superintendent regarding parent/Booster calls he's been getting supporting the reputation of Sports Warehouse. I still remember the trouble when we questioned the hotel bill for the team and the cheerleaders when they went to the state championship game two years ago. Fred and his coaches riled up the Booster Club and even the superintendent sided with them. Even though I still think that we were right, I got clobbered and was lucky to keep my job. But, on the other hand, we still can't ignore a possible lawsuit from another vendor."

"They all but threatened it!" interrupted Tom.

"Lastly, when all is said and done we *do* need these helmets in time for the season and Sports Warehouse is the only one that can get them done in time, and the Booster Club *is* pitching in the balance," pursued Al.

"Aw, that's bull, Al, and you know it. The other vendors can provide enough helmets in our school colors to make up for the ones that got ruined. No, they won't be the same or as fancy, but they'll match just fine. *And*, if the Boosters want to help so much, then they can have a fundraiser at the games to raise money for *all* the helmets next year. Heck, they'll have a perfect angle by pointing out how they are not all the same. They can milk the tragedy of the flood."

Al leaned back in his chair and contemplated whether he should cancel the purchase order to Sports Warehouse and rebid the contract for the helmets properly.

Questions for Discussion

1. What are the legal issues in this dilemma?
2. Should school district officials owe a sense of loyalty to vendors who have treated them well? Why or why not? If they do, should this loyalty supersede "technicalities" in the law?
3. Is giving preferential treatment to vendors who have done well for the school fair to those vendors who are interested in doing business but have not done so in the past? Is there an obligation to the community? If so, what?
4. Is giving preferential treatment to some vendors over others an abuse of power? Would your answer be any different if you found out that all the vendors a district used were white-male owned and operated while other equally competent minority and female vendors were ignored?
5. What would the profession expect the SBO to do in this case?
6. What action would be in the best interest of the students? Explain the rationale for your answer.
7. What would you do if you were Al? Explain the rationale for your decision from an ethical perspective.

CASE 7: THE NEW BUSINESS MANAGER AND THE PTO TREASURER

Maria, the business manager of Granite Ridge School District, was starting her second year with the district. Her training and background were in banking, and she recently had relocated to the district from a small community north of Granite Ridge. One of her new responsibilities was to do internal audits of several district funds and, by board policy, to obtain and review financial reports from the treasurers of the district's parent–teacher organizations (PTOs).

Because of staff turnover and other more pressing items, the PTO reports and books had not been looked at for three or more years. Maria sent out a notice to the principals requesting each school's PTO books, reports, and backup documentation for the past two years, and within a week all but one school had complied. The principal of that school called Janet, the PTO treasurer, and found out that she would be out of town for a few days. Janet's husband said he would box up the PTO records in her desk and drop them off the next day, which he did.

The Dilemma

It only took the next morning to get through the other PTO books because of the apparent order and care taken with the financial records. Janet's records, however, were another story. The first simple test Maria applied—to reconcile revenue recordings in the ledger to bank deposits—did not add up. The records appeared to all be there; however, things were in such a state of disarray that it was hard to follow what Janet had done. Some things were recorded; some things were not. A couple of the transactions were really vague and she photocopied them with the idea of getting back to them later. Maria set the boxes aside, called the principal, and asked if she could set up a time to review the records with both the principal and Janet.

When the principal called the house, Janet answered the phone. The principal began to explain what Maria needed to do, and he could hear Janet speaking to her husband about the "boxes" he took to the school. Janet was obviously agitated and told the principal that her records were not in any kind of order for someone to review and that she would go to the central office herself this afternoon. When Janet arrived, Maria was tied up in a meeting.

Janet asked to have her boxes with the records returned to her and Sally, Maria's secretary, thinking Maria was done with the information, readily handed them over. When Maria came back from her meeting, she was more than a little direct with Sally about giving back the files.

"Sally, in the future you must not turn over records without my explicit instruction or awareness. My audit on those records not only was incomplete, but had disturbing discrepancies that I need to address with Mrs. Purnell [Janet]," instructed Maria curtly.

"Well, I can hardly believe," responded Sally, "that there would be any *real* problems with the records. Why, Janet has lived in the community all of her life. Her husband runs a local charity foundation and Janet teaches Sunday school! I understand we have policies, but I am quite sure you are mistaken if you are implying anything improper with Janet's handling of the PTO funds. Also, I don't think anyone around the district would appreciate such implications either. Janet is related to two board members and her husband plays golf with the superintendent."

"Nonetheless, Sally, I *need* those records, and it was improper for her to take them without meeting with me as requested. Please follow protocol in the future regardless of the individual," Maria reiterated.

Maria called the principal and let him know that she wanted the school's PTO records back as soon as possible. The principal did not seem alarmed and, if anything, was agitated by Maria's pressing the issue. Janet had been in the PTO for the past seven years as her three children attended the school.

The principal explained, "I'm sure Janet probably just wants to put the books in order so that you can get through them. She's probably embarrassed about how they look." The principal added, "I know she sounded furious with her husband for giving them to you in that state."

Once Maria heard that, her experience and training told her that there was likely more to this issue, but now she did not have records to pursue her instinct. Maria told the principal to please call Janet and set a three-day deadline to return the files. The principal called and left a message on the answering machine.

Two weeks later, the files had not been returned. Maria had left several of her own messages on Janet's answering machine to no avail. The principal had once again told Maria that this was not an issue and that Janet was a trusted parent and valued contributor to his school.

Maria then let her superintendent know what was going on, but the superintendent directly informed Maria, "No accusations will be made unless I make them based on overwhelming evidence." The superintendent also informed Maria that he had already heard from the building principal about this matter and that Maria had better be careful or be very right about any suspicions. "In addition," he said gruffly, "one of the board members has already inquired as to what this issue is with your harassing Janet. I really don't like the idea of your getting a reputation like that in our community so soon after your hiring. Please resolve this issue quickly."

The Decision Point

Halfway through the third week, Sally brought all of Janet's records into the office. She had seen Janet at a function the night before and Janet asked her to please stop at the house to pick them up and "go make your boss happy." Maria spent several hours reviewing the records. They were spotless, precise, and the most recent bank account statement reconciled to the penny. However, there were a lot of things that she had seen in the boxes before that were now missing. She was sure that her chances of ever seeing them were pretty remote. She remembered her photocopy of a suspicious transaction and pulled it out. It was pretty clear that this transaction was not represented in the cleaned up set of books. While that fact made her even more suspicious, it certainly was not going to be enough to continue any investigation. Maria was under enough pressure as it was to leave Janet alone.

She felt stumped and stared at the two records in front of her. Then Maria noticed that on her photocopy there were some banking information and transaction numbers, both of which were from the bank where she had formerly worked. On a whim, she called one of her former banking peers with whom she had a long-established professional relationship. After exchanging normal pleasantries, she briefly explained that she had some suspicions about banking activities "at the district" and asked if he could take a look to see if anything looked irregular at their end.

Within several minutes, Maria's friend told her that there was definitely activity occurring between a personal account and the school's PTO account. It included (amazingly) several split deposits between the two, which should not have been allowed by the tellers.

Maria's friend at the bank, realizing that he may have stepped into something, said to Maria, "If anybody asks, you didn't get this here!"

Questions for Discussion

1. What are the legal issues in this dilemma? What legal responsibility does Maria have, assuming that she strongly suspected, but could not prove, wrongdoing on Janet's part? Was there any legal problem with Maria's using her connections to find out more about Janet's financial records? Why or why not? Even if Maria's actions in obtaining information from her old bank were wrong, and assuming Janet is guilty, do the ends justify the means?

2. What is the fair course of action for Maria to take?

3. What is the most caring course of action? Do you believe Maria was caring towards Janet? Why or why not?

4. Several people in this situation have varying degrees of power. Who are they and what is the scope of their power? Did any of these persons abuse their power?

5. What would the profession expect Maria to do? Did she meet professional expectations? Exceed them?

6. What actions should Maria take in relation to Janet, the PTO, and/or the school that would be in the best interests of the students?

7. What impact might Maria's decision have on the community? Should she consider the needs of the community in making her decision? Why or why not?

8. What would you do if you were in Maria's place?

CASE 8: SUPPORT YOUR LOCAL BANK

Superintendent Harry Richards had been with the Hawk Mountain District for many years. He was a highly respected member of the community and widely regarded by district personnel as an all-around nice guy who could be approached about anything, ranging from unruly students to trouble at home. Harry Richards had seen the community through a number of tough times that would have sent less dedicated superintendents scrambling for the hills. As a popular and well-known community leader, he attended many social functions that included community business leaders.

By contrast, the business manager, Susan Fletcher, was relatively new to the district and to the community. Susan was a recent but very experienced transplant from a much larger school district in one of the more urban communities to the south. She was hired to update and modernize the business office and services. Both the board and the superintendent had made clear their expectations that she should use her experience and expertise to help the district save money and become more efficient.

The Dilemma

In order to achieve these goals, Susan began reviewing the practices in the business office. Her first area was banking services. She found that the district dealt exclusively with Alpha Bank, a local financial institution. Further study indicated that the district's general fund used two primary bank accounts for disbursements: the general account for all miscellaneous cash and check receipts, disbursements to vendors, and overnight investment transactions, and the payroll account, which received funds transferred from the general account to cover all payroll transactions. Additionally, the district had other accounts for student activities, dental/vision escrow, food service, athletic, foundation, and capital reserve funds.

With this background she initiated an online search of the Electronic Resource Center of best practices in school business management maintained by the Pennsylvania Association of School Business Officials. There she found a best practice listing for a request for proposal for banking services. This best-practice RFP seemed to be just what she was seeking:

> The objectives of this request for proposal are to identify the banking institution that can offer the highest quality service at the best value to the organization. The District intends to maximize deposit availability, maximize deposit security, and minimize cost and management time. As you will see when you review this proposal, the District is interested in obtaining the best mix of services to meet our specific banking needs. . . .

An important aspect of this proposal is to obtain market rates (federal fund rates) of interest on all funds held in our accounts with limited associated risks.

The District will evaluate each proposal received based on the following criteria:

- Creditworthiness
- Investment of Funds
- Cost and Flexibility of Services
- Ability to Provide Services Efficiently and Effectively through Automation
- Funds Deposited and Collateralized in Accordance with all Federal, State and Local Laws, and in accordance with the further limitations in this request as they relate to collateralization requirements
- References from other governmental clients
- Bank Branch proximity to District Office
- All banks submitting proposals must have a branch geographically located in the District
- Interest rate and/or earnings credit rate paid on all time deposit accounts
- Overall best value for the District as determined by the District

The best practice RFP gave detailed specifications in the areas of collection services, disbursement services, monthly reporting, electronic services, investment services, and courier services, which identified the considerations in choosing an appropriate bank that could serve all the district's needs in a cost-effective manner.

As Susan compared the current banking agreement, she realized that the local bank the district used was not providing many of the services that are typically offered by other larger institutions. Further, the interest rate provided to the school district was, in her opinion, unusually low. As a precursor to an attempt to improve the banking services received by the district and to earn better interest on investments, Susan made a preliminary comparison of banking rates and available services from Alpha Bank and two statewide banks with branch offices in the district.

The comparison was striking; the local bank offered fewer services and its rates were noticeably higher. Happy with the possibility of receiving more and better services at lower cost, Susan eagerly presented her financial findings to the superintendent. A key recommendation in her report was that the district should put out an RFP for banking services and select the best offer from the banks that responded. She clearly expected that the district would be motivated to change financial institutions.

The Decision Point

The superintendent, after looking at the fruits of Susan's labor, was completely opposed to any change regarding the financial arrangements of the district. Harry reminded her that in a small community everyone must work together and support one another. He told her that the bank sponsored a dinner for the administration and school board during the holidays and provided money in scholarships to graduating students who agreed to open an account. As further incentive, employees of the district who had an account at this bank received an additional 0.25 percent reduction on their mortgage rates. It was clear that buying local was more important to him than improved, lower cost services.

Susan was disappointed with the response she received and, now determined to prove her findings beneficial to the school district, continued her investigations. She expanded her preliminary comparisons to obtain the latest rates and services from Alpha Bank and from several more statewide banks, as well. The findings only strengthened her conviction that substantial cost savings could be obtained by making the banking services contract more competitive. After all, this was what she had been hired to do.

On the other hand, her superintendent knew the community inside and out and had the trust of its citizens. She could understand that changing banks might hurt some of the carefully built relationships and have repercussions on the support of the business community and to the district itself. However, this cozy local banking arrangement was costing the district money.

Questions for Discussion

1. Are there legal implications to resolving this dilemma? If so, what are they?
2. Are there issues of fairness here? If so, to whom do they apply and why?
3. Are there issues of caring to which Susan needs to attend? To whom do they apply? Why? Does Susan owe a duty of care to people working in the local bank? If, so what is this? If not, why not?

4. Is there an abuse of power in this situation? If so, who is abusing power and how?
5. What course of action would be in the best interests of the students? Why?
6. What ethical issues arise with either including or ignoring the needs of the community in Susan's decision making?
7. If you were in Susan's place, what would you do?

8

FACILITY, PROPERTY, AND INFORMATION MANAGEMENT

Management of facilities, property acquisition, and technology-based information are three important and distinct areas articulated in the ASBO standards. This chapter focuses on dilemmas illustrating the ethical dimensions surrounding these issues. The first case addresses financial services related to a bond issue for new building construction. The second is concerned with selling a school that has historical significance. The third focuses on management of computer systems and ethical issues that can arise in relation to ownership of software developed by school personnel.

CASE 9: INVESTMENT ADVISERS

The administration and the board of school directors at Thaberville Area School District realized that construction of a new elementary school building was becoming inevitable. District enrollment was growing steadily and increased residential development in the district's outlying areas was noticeable during the past several years. The district superintendent, Dr. Frank Mariwell, was well connected in the local community and had been evaluating potential locations for the new facility. Together with the rest of the administrative team, including Ms. Barbara Zoltek, the district's chief financial officer, Mariwell selected an appropriate site for the new school.

Ms. Zoltek was assigned the lead role for the fiscal aspects of the new elementary school building project and was expected to report to the board periodically with her findings and recommendations. The planning process for this facility was proceeding on schedule and preliminary cost projections estimated the cost of the new facility at $20 million. The next step was to evaluate the debt service required to support this construction project. She knew that a good financial adviser was needed to construct a debt service schedule that would be acceptable to the board and the taxpayers. In addition, the district's policies required that proposals be solicited for such a large financial commitment. After identifying three possible firms for the project, the district requested proposals from each of the potential investment advisers.

Separate meetings were scheduled with the investment companies to review their proposals. The Bonderman Group and Grant, Foster & Gockley (GFG) were full-service investment firms that would serve as lead underwriters of the debt. MSI Associates, the third investment company, would act as an investment adviser and assist the district in holding a public auction to offer this debt. Each of the three firms visited the district and met with Dr. Mariwell and Ms. Zoltek to discuss the specifics.

Following the presentation of the three proposals, Ms. Zoltek took the information and put it into comparative form as shown in table 8.1. The key fiscal indicators for the district were the net proceeds from the bond issue (total issue amount less fees for the investment adviser) and the total repayment cost for the district. On both measures MSI was the best choice. It had a lower fee than either of the other two firms, since it was only managing the bond auction and not underwriting the bond issue. Likewise, the district would have lower total repayment costs with MSI (and Bonderman), due primarily to a two-year shorter repayment period. In comparison with MSI, it would cost $150,000 more in adviser fees and $2,274,000 in total repayment costs if the district used GFG, and $50,000 more in adviser fees and $82,500 in total repayment costs if it used Bonderman. Although not shown on the table, the debt service costs for the first several years were quite similar for all three firms.

These facts made it clear to Ms. Zoltek that she should recommend the MSI proposal. If the board were not comfortable with the moderate uncertainty surrounding the auction process, then the Bonderman proposal would be her back-up recommendation. She scheduled a private meeting with the superintendent to review her findings and have him endorse this recommendation to the board.

"Dr. Mariwell, good morning," she said as she entered his office. "I have put together a recommendation for the board meeting this week and created a simple chart that I think will clarify things for board members in viewing the different proposals. As you can see, without a doubt the MSI firm is going to be the best choice for the district. I realize this board has not had firsthand experience with the auction process, but I worked with auctions in my previous district and they turned out very well. Also, I made a brief presentation to the board this fall about the process, since there were several informative sessions on this topic at the last ASBO conference. Though it is relatively new, I think we can show them that the process can be quite beneficial." She smiled and waited for his expected reply.

After reviewing the chart, he looked at her and said, "We will be recommending Grant, Foster & Gockley. It is a reputable investment firm that has been around for a long time. It has served us very well in the past and will do so again this time."

Ms. Zoltek knew this was not the right decision and tried to contest his conclusion. "I'm not sure I understand, Dr. Mariwell. I realize that

Table 8.1. Ms. Zoltek's Three Proposals

	Comparison of Proposals		
	MSI	Bonderman	GFG
Amount of issue	$20,000,000	$20,000,000	$20,000,000
Investment adviser costs	$650,000	$700,000	$800,000
Net proceeds	$19,350,000	$19,300,000	$19,200,000
Rank	1	2	3
Difference from best proposal		($50,000)	($150,000)
Total repayment	$34,532,500	$34,615,000	$36,806,500
Rank	1	2	3
Difference from best proposal		($82,500)	($2,274,000)

we have used Grant, Foster & Gockley in the past, and yes, the district has been pleased with their work, but in this case, I think I must reiterate my recommendation. In fact, I cannot even conscientiously recommend Grant, Foster & Gockley as the second choice with the proposal it presented."

Dr. Mariwell responded, "Grant, Foster & Gockley is our firm and will be recommended to the board to underwrite this debt." The superintendent stood up and it was clear the meeting was over.

The Dilemma

Ms. Zoltek returned to her office and thought about what had transpired. She realized that Dr. Mariwell would not allow a presentation to the board evaluating alternative proposals at a level of detail that would show the additional financial costs of using GFG. She also realized that the board would probably accept his choice without serious questions. However, she felt uncomfortable that the district would be expending greater funds in securing this debt than necessary without even knowing it.

Ms. Zoltek knew that GFG held a gala overnight event annually at a posh resort and that Dr. Mariwell and his spouse were always invited to this event. Also, the superintendent was the recipient of numerous holiday gifts from this firm and was invited to several dinners throughout the course of the year. Dr. Mariwell accepted all these gifts personally and attended all of these events. After all, he had some very close associations with the senior management of this company and enjoyed spending time with them at the local country club. On the other hand, she knew the district had done business with the other two firms and, although she guessed not, she wondered if they accorded Dr. Mariwell similar treatment.

The Decision Point

Ms. Zoltek meditated on these facts. She *knew* that MSI had the best proposal. To recommend someone else would be a violation of her professional responsibilities and values. However, if she did not recommend the firm of Grant, Foster & Gockley, it would certainly result in a serious conflict with Dr. Mariwell and could be seen as insubordination; it would also jeopardize her job. Even if Dr. Mariwell made the presentation to the board, she was worried how she should respond if the board asked for her opinion. An honest answer could result in a public conflict between her and the superintendent and possibly disturb the amicable relationship between the board and the district administration. She had only a short time to decide what to do since the board meeting was in three days.

Questions for Discussion

1. What legal issues does this case present relative to accepting bids? If Ms. Zoltek accepts Dr. Mariwell's decision, would she be in violation of the law? Why or why not?
2. In light of the three bids, what is the fair decision?
3. What is the most caring decision Ms. Zoltek could make here? Does caring extend to loyalty to the superintendent? Does it extend to loyalty to vendors who take good care of their clients?
4. How is power exerted in this situation? Is there an abuse of power? Explain your answer.
5. What would the profession expect of Ms. Zoltek in this situation?
6. Is there a "best interests of the students" issue in this scenario? An issue related to the community? If so, what are they? If not, why not?
7. What would you do if you were Ms. Zoltek? Explain the rationale for your decision from an ethical perspective.

CASE 10: THE HISTORIC SCHOOL

Since 1925, the venerable Fairview School had stood on a city street up the hill a short distance from the city center. A Greek Revival design, its handsome facade was a proud landmark, and generations of students had attended class in its high-ceilinged spaces, sitting at oak desks, sunlight flooding through the generous windows. With marble floors in the hallways and graceful proportions throughout, Fairview embodied the era's concept of a place of learning, a place in which education should occur, a place of dignity to surround the enterprise and match the high value in which education was held.

Times change. The proximity of the school to downtown took its toll. The residential area around the school was encroached on by businesses, and the large houses from the early 1900s, when not torn down, became divided into apartments. Families moved to other residential areas. Originally a high school, Fairview became an elementary school when a new high school was built. By the mid-1990s, the school was no longer in use, except for a few community classes in the evenings. Then these activities also were terminated.

As well as the neighborhood altering over the intervening years, many renovations and "modernization" efforts had been effected inside the building. Ceilings were artificially lowered, classrooms cut into smaller units, walls covered with paneling. By the time the last class of children left Fairview, it was no longer recognizable, at least on the inside, as the elegant, distinguished building it had been.

The school district pondered what to do with Fairview School. With the combination of a small but vocal citizens group protesting a rise in taxes and an increase in expenses owing to new state mandates, the school board was interested in exploring various solutions and their fiscal impacts on the district. The business manager was directed to prepare a report on the possibilities for the old building and to make recommendations.

The Dilemma

As the business manager began studying various scenarios, it was clear that selling the property to a developer who would then tear down the school to build on the site yielded the greatest amount of money to the district. Several developers had contacted the district periodically to inquire about the Fairview School site. However, city zoning ordinances, as they presently stood, limited the use of the site to educational or public buildings. The business manager, when he contacted the zoning officer, learned that changing zoning laws could be difficult, would necessitate some strong arguments before the city council, and might go counter to state regulations on land use. But a change could be attempted, and an aggressive developer would certainly try. On the other hand, the zoning officer told him, the city council was looking for a means of expanding the city library and had recently asked him what he thought the school district was going to do about Fairview School. The zoning officer suggested that a tour be made of the school site, including the interior of the building itself, to ascertain its condition and potential for development.

On the day of the tour, the zoning officer brought along several persons who had an interest in Fairview School, including a member of the city council and the president of the local historical society. The business manager had with him a member of the school board and an architect who had worked on various school projects.

It was the first time the business manager or anyone else in the group had actually been in the school. Expecting to be appalled by the condition of the building, they were surprised to find mostly neglect, not widespread damage and decay. The architect began to point out how some of the prior modernization effects could be reversed, the school board member asked whether the gym could be restored, the city councilwoman talked about available grants for restoration projects, particularly for adapting it for use as a public library. The business manager himself started to link Fairview with an alternative high school, which had lately been proposed. As he and the board member discussed this possibility, the president of the historical society recalled hearing that during the 1930s a mural had been painted, under the auspices of the Depression-era Works Progress Administration, in the entrance hall of the old high school. With some careful exploration and judicious prying, one of the 1960s panels was removed, revealing a small portion of a bold, colorful, beautifully executed painting depicting the history of the community.

A week later at the next school board meeting, the room was packed. Thanks to an article in the local newspaper about Fairview's history, word of the possibility of Fairview School being razed had gotten around the community, and dozens of people had requested the opportunity to address the matter. From elderly alumni in wheelchairs to those who were in the last Fairview class, from neighborhood advocates to members of the local historical society, and from several state officials knowledgeable and eloquent in historic preservation, the school board listened to their concerns. Memories of school days were aired, the importance of Fairview to the integrity of the old neighborhood was stressed. Schemes for reuse of the building were proposed. The mural was described as a priceless treasure; the possible loss to the community of the school itself was compared to the destruction of the famed Pennsylvania Station in New York City.

The Decision Point

The board responded by reiterating that while no decision had been made, it had the responsibility to balance students' educational needs with their fiduciary responsibilities to the district. One member noted that money was increasingly scarce at the present time and, without a tax increase, programs might have to be cut. The board chair stated that a report with recommendations prepared by the business manager would be presented at the next board meeting in two weeks, and it would be influential in their decision. As all eyes in the room turned toward him, the business manager realized that his report could have considerable repercussions, not only on the financial status of the district and the fate of Fairview School but on the broader issue of preserving the community's history.

Questions for Discussion

1. What legal issues are illustrated by this dilemma? Are they relevant to the outcome? If not, why not? If they are relevant, explain why they matter.
2. If the school business administrator must balance the historical benefits of saving Fairview School against badly needed financial resources for the district, what would be the fair decision? How would the SBO make this decision in light of the greater good for the greater number?
3. Is there a caring aspect to the SBO's dilemma? If so, what is it and how would it influence the final decision?
4. Who has the power in this situation? How might the issue of power determine the outcome?
5. Discuss the various possible outcomes in light of what is in the best interests of the students. Which outcome would most benefit the students? Why?

6. What is the community's stake in the outcome? Should this stake influence the business manager's decision? Why or why not?
7. What would you do if you were the business manager? Explain the rationale for your decision from an ethical perspective.

CASE 11: SOFTWARE OWNERSHIP

The Gates Union School District recently experienced rapid growth in student enrollment, an expanded athletic program, formation of a recreation association, and a general overall increase in traffic and use of the district's facilities. As a result, the district had problems such as double scheduling of spaces, unclean spaces, spaces not properly prepared for use, and doors locked to those approved to use spaces, all of which caused great frustration to the district and those using the facilities.

In response, Andrew Carlisle, the supervisor of custodial services, approached Mark Nittany, the business manager, for approval to investigate the implementation of an automated facility usage system. A single district-wide schedule would be crucial to inform all staff of what and when facilities were being used. Such a schedule would support staff and facility users, and minimize the number of facility usage conflicts. The system would reduce paperwork and become a districtwide tool for the scheduling of all activities.

Some of the scheduling confusion resulted from reliance on the past technology coordinator's promise to design some kind of scheduling calendar. This person left suddenly to take a higher-paying job in the private sector and left several important jobs unfinished, including the calendar for facility usage. The coordinator promised to complete them on his own time, but they were never done. There were other important district projects that also were left undone in the process, some as critical as attendance and grade reporting at the high school.

The district quickly mobilized a search for a new technology coordinator to find someone qualified *and* willing to work in the district for the coordinator's salary, which was considerably less than offered in industry (a difference of a range of $10,000 to $30,000 per year). Finally Gates Union School District discovered and hired Curtis Smith. In his interview, he mentioned that having less pressure, less travel, more autonomy to work on his own projects, and being able to design unique programs for the district without interference from competitive colleagues would be a relief to him.

Smith was seen as a boon to the district. He had been in the industry long enough to be familiar with the older technology and programs the district owned, but also knew the newer technologies that existed for educational institutions. As a matter of fact, that was his strong point, since he had worked for an endowed organization that developed software and consulted with schools across the country. He also ran a small consulting service. During the hiring process, he asked to be able to continue limited private consulting on the side when it did not interfere or conflict with his duties in the district. The district agreed.

Within two years, Smith became invaluable, bringing to the job an extensive knowledge of data networks and computers. He quickly became the only staff member with an understanding of the district's network and how it operated. He finished nearly all of the past technology coordinator's projects, completed and improved the attendance and grade reporting systems, and saved the district a tremendous amount of money, especially in reprogramming costs. Parents noticed too, as they would often make comments that the new interactive district website was "neat" and "useful." Smith had taken over a fledgling technology department at a time when technology had become a focus for most school districts and had done an outstanding job in bringing it "up to speed."

As the technology coordinator, Curtis Smith reported to the assistant superintendent of instructional services, Mike Pearson, while Andrew Carlisle, the supervisor of custodial services, reported to Mark Nittany, the business manager. The relationship between Nittany and Smith had always been positive, since earlier Nittany had spearheaded the efforts to install a districtwide computer backbone necessary for a district network. While the district's network was created before Smith arrived, he knew of the business manager's involvement with that project and he viewed the business manager as a champion of technology in the district. As a result, he consulted with Nittany on financial and infrastructure-related questions.

The business manager suggested that Carlisle approach Smith to see if he could provide a low-cost automated solution to the ongoing scheduling problems with district facilities. Nittany was aware of a calendar/

schedule program that Smith had developed, and he encouraged the supervisor of custodial services to pursue the matter in more detail with Smith. The automated calendar already developed by Smith was very basic and would need considerable revision to make it useful as a districtwide calendar. The effort to develop the system would concentrate on making the basic calendar more "user friendly," so that all employees might log on to the system to make "reservations" without any double bookings or other confusion.

Following Nittany's request, Carlisle approached Smith about developing a facility usage schedule (FUS) to document the use of the district's many facilities. Smith enthusiastically agreed to take on the project and offered to do whatever was necessary to develop a user-friendly, effective system. Several meetings took place between Smith and Carlisle, with the central office and building secretaries, principals, and athletic director, to outline the critical areas of communications and needs for such a system. Smith stressed that he had already developed a generic calendar system and would need everyone's considerable input to refine it to fit the needs as defined by each staff member involved with facility scheduling. The business manager sat in on some of the initial meetings to help evaluate the potential of designing an in-house system.

As a result of this collaborative approach, Smith developed the new system based on input from not only the supervisor of custodial services and his staff but also district and school building administrators, as well as secretaries. Since it was being written and developed in-house, the new program was constantly being refined into the current program. Throughout the development process, district staff continually provided opinions, suggestions, and requests to improve the program. To Smith's credit, most of this input was acted on and incorporated into the new facility usage schedule software program.

The Dilemma

Andrew Carlisle regularly attended regional chapter meetings of the Facility Management Administrators Association, where he commented on the district's efforts to develop its own facility usage schedule. Districts often shared ideas that might prove helpful to others, and the sharing of FUS was presented in that vein. Other school districts voiced an interest in looking at the district's system because a company that had provided similar facility-related modules to districts in this region had recently closed.

After a year of successful operation, Curtis Smith approached Mark Nittany with a request for the district to recognize his ownership of FUS in a written agreement. Curtis arrived for his meeting with Mark and entered the office casually. "Hi, Mark," he said, "I have some paperwork here that I need you to take a look at and possibly take to the board. It has to do with the formal recognition of my ownership of the FUS program I've been working on all year. All of the writing of the program, by the way, was done outside of the normal work day at my home."

"Oh . . . let's take a look," answered Mark with some confusion. After reading it over, Mark was even more puzzled as to the district's role or stance on this matter. "This is a highly unusual request, Curtis. Not only is there no district policy on how to respond to such an agreement, but there's nothing similar in our district's history to guide us. I think it will take some time to study this agreement and our policies before you will get a response. I hope you weren't looking for one soon?" Mark explained.

"Well, yes," Curtis replied, "actually, I was hoping for no more than two weeks, as I am looking to expand FUS to provide increased functions beyond just the district's current needs."

Rubbing his chin, Mark hesitated, "The best I can say for now is that I will submit this request to the superintendent today, and the soonest any formal action can be taken on this agreement is at the next board meeting."

"Okay," Curtis shrugged, "but if you could please get back to me in the meantime with the superintendent's thoughts, I'd surely appreciate it."

"Will do, Curtis," answered Mark. As Curtis left, Mark sat with the agreement still in his hands, thinking about what just happened and how he should present this request to the superintendent, let alone the board. First, he thought he would call the assistant superintendent of instructional services, Mike Pearson. "Hello, Mike," he said, "Mark here. We've got a potential problem regarding ownership of some of the software that Curtis Smith has developed for us. Can we meet this afternoon?" He also called the superintendent, Jeannette Cox, to see if she was available as well.

The Decision Point

Prior to the meeting regarding the ownership agreement being sought by Smith, the assistant superintendent had gone to Smith's website and found information promoting the facility usage schedule system with an actual demo utilizing the district's calendar data. The promotional information included fees to purchase and install the facility usage schedule. In addition, other software solutions were being marketed as well, including a maintenance work order system, which was currently being developed with district staff. At the meeting, the assistant superintendent described what he had seen on the website.

The business manager reported that recently the supervisor of custodial services had made several requests to Smith for program refinements to the FUS, but he refused to make the programming changes associated with the district's request.

"Well, gentlemen, what are our options?" Jeanette Cox asked.

"Personally, I think we are in a bind," answered the assistant superintendent. "On one hand, we have a district program developed and used in-house—yet the blueprints of that program were based on the skeleton he had when he came. Then we have the added problem of promising him he *could* do some private consulting and work for the district at the same time and he claims he did most of the work on FUS on his own time."

"Yes, but," Mark interrupted, "his work is not to *conflict* with his job here with us. I tried calling him twice these past weeks and he was out of his office. I've never had trouble reaching Curtis before. Then I found out by strong implication from the secretaries that he was out of the office because he was running workshops for neighboring districts—I'd call that conflicting, wouldn't you?"

"Okay, Mark, but where is your policy?" Mike countered. "I agree that it seems fishy, but we didn't get in writing a definition of what constitutes conflict and what constitutes consulting, and we have absolutely *nothing* in our policies on the intellectual property rights that he's claiming."

"We *do* have a policy in our district employee handbook that describes how personal days and sick days are and are not supposed to be used. Can't we use that? Also, he does charge other districts for the program that *we* funded to create. Although it's not a lot of revenue the district would give up, if we just roll over on this, it sets a bad precedent. What do you say, Jeanette? Ever have anything like this in your old district?" Mark asked.

"Actually, no" she replied. "But one very important point the two of you have missed is the fact that this man is a huge asset to our district, and pursuing either a denial *or* a disciplinary action could likely result in his leaving. One thing I *have* observed in other districts is how rarely a techie can relate to administration, teachers, children, *and* parents, and Curtis does that in spades. We need to ask ourselves if we are willing to lose a person like that over this issue. Also, don't forget how much we all rely on him and that so much of what he does for us is custom designed—will someone else we bring in be able to run it or even figure it out? So I ask you two again, what are our options?"

Questions for Discussion

1. What are the legal issues in this case? From the district's perspective? From Curtis's perspective?
2. What would be a fair resolution of this dilemma? For the district? For Curtis?
3. Are there issues of caring in this dilemma? What are they and how would you apply them?
4. Who has the power in this situation? How might power be used or abused in resolving this dilemma?
5. What are the implications of this dilemma for the community?
6. What resolution might be in the best interests of students?
7. What would you do if you were Mark Nittany? Explain the rationale for your decision from an ethical perspective.

9

ANCILLARY SERVICES: TRANSPORTATION

Ancillary services include risk management, transportation, and food service. The three dilemmas represented in this chapter involve transportation issues. Indeed, these types of situations predominated among the ones our contributors submitted. Part of this concern may be attributed to the great deal of time SBOs spend on transportation-related issues, the huge sums of money often needed to subsidize transportation costs (especially in rural and/or isolated areas), and the inherent difficulty of problems related to transportation.

The three cases below illustrate the complexity and variety of ethical issues that can and often do arise. The first deals with a request to establish a special bus stop, the second addresses creating a new and different bus stop based on the demands of an influential parent, and the third raises racial and religious concerns associated with transporting private school students.

CASE 12: SPECIAL BUS STOP

Brad Barnes stopped in the office of his boss, Amy Thompson, the business manager, at the end of the day on a Thursday afternoon. In his twenty years as transportation coordinator for the Glen View School District, few transportation situations arose that he had not encountered before and even fewer that he had not been able to resolve on his own. However, over the years he increasingly noted a trend of parent demands for more transportation services. The philosophy of the Glen View School District was to accommodate requests from working parents for bus stops at the homes of baby-sitters whenever possible. However, any accommodations needed to be made within the confines of running a cost-effective transportation operation and in compliance with the regulations of the state Department of Education and Department of Transportation (DOT).

In the three years Brad had been working with Amy Thompson, they had developed a good relationship. He knew that she appreciated his efforts to handle most problems independently, but she expected open communication from him, especially when it involved letting her know when a parent might be planning to go over his head and request contact with his supervisor. Brad respected Thompson's management style and the fact that she typically backed up his decisions in such cases.

Earlier in the day, Brad asked Mrs. Thompson if he could speak with her for a few minutes to provide background for a call she was likely to receive from Mr. Starner, the grandfather of a second grade student. Since the start of the school year, Brad had received several calls from Mr. Starner requesting a bus stop in front of his granddaughter's home. In reviewing the request, Brad determined that the walking distance from the girl's home to the school was approximately one-half mile, well within the state guidelines and district policy for walking distance for an elementary student. The walking route was not a hazardous one as determined by the DOT, and any transportation services would not be eligible for state subsidy. Anticipating a barrage of similar requests from like-minded and emboldened parents, Brad denied Starner's request for the bus stop.

Brad related these basic details about the request to Mrs. Thompson. He also shared his thoughts about Starner's reasons for requesting the transportation services. Starner had told Brad that his son and daughter-in-law, the child's parents and both physicians at the local county hospital, generally left for work in the morning before the child walked to school. Starner had been driving from a neighboring town each morning to provide child care for his granddaughter. It was Brad's impression that the grandfather was tired of these arrangements and a bus stop at the home, together with the time the bus took to get to school, would conveniently provide early morning child care for his granddaughter.

The Dilemma

The next morning, true to Brad's prediction, Amy Thompson received a telephone call from Mr. Starner. She was pleased that she had gotten Brad's assessment of the issues in advance and was prepared to back up his position. However, Mr. Starner added some new information to support his request for transportation services. Two years ago, his son and daughter-in-law lost their oldest child in an accident as he was walking to school. Apparently a truck struck the ten-year-old boy as he crossed a busy intersection on the way to school in another district. Mr. Starner was adamant that the walking route his granddaughter traveled daily was similar to the one that claimed the life of his only grandson, and was therefore unsafe. He stated that his granddaughter must cross a street with speeding cars at the busiest time of the day. His own health did not permit him to accompany her on the walk.

Mr. Starner had observed that a bus went by the house in the morning and stopped a few blocks away to pick up "that boy in the wheelchair." After all, claimed Mr. Starner, "that boy is practically next door to the school and the bus picks him up." Mr. Starner demanded that, in the interest of the safety of his only remaining grandchild, an additional stop be created. He accused the school district of negligence and disregard for the safety of his granddaughter.

Further, Mr. Starner claimed that his granddaughter, who wore a headscarf for religious reasons, has been the focus of harassment while walking to school due to anti-Muslim sentiment. He contended that this little girl should not have to endure taunts from school bullies. He closed his part of the conversation by challenging Mrs. Thompson to check out the walking route herself.

The Decision Point

Mrs. Thompson had handled her share of angry telephone calls. She patiently listened to Starner's litany of reasons why a bus stop should be added. She was mindful of Brad's opinion about Starner's ulterior motive and believed it had merit. However, she could readily appreciate the sensitive nature of the apparent sources of Mr. Starner's concern and did not immediately dismiss his request. Mrs. Thompson did not take accusations concerning safety lightly and her intuition told her to proceed cautiously with this one. She agreed to investigate the situation further but laid the groundwork for denying the request by explaining the regulations and procedures used by the school district for establishing bus stops.

Mrs. Thompson and Brad both observed the route on several different mornings during the times when elementary students walked to school. They did not notice a high volume of traffic. Mrs. Thompson directed Brad to contact the DOT to review the concerns expressed by Starner. When he did, he learned that a traffic study had recently been conducted and the route was identified as nonhazardous. The DOT did not feel that further study was warranted.

Questions for Discussion

1. What are the legal issues in this dilemma? How much discretion do Brad Barnes and Amy Thompson have relative to legal restrictions in this matter?

2. What is the fair course of action relative to Mr. Starner and his granddaughter? The other students in the school district? How would you resolve this dilemma based on the greater good for the greater number?

3. What is the most caring course of action relative to Mr. Starner? Relative to his granddaughter?

4. Who is in the least powerful position in this scenario? Who has the power in this situation? How might this power be used to result in a just decision?

5. How would the profession expect Amy Thompson to act? Was she acting in a professional manner? Why or why not?

6. What decision would be in the best interests of Mr. Starner's granddaughter? In the best interests of the other students?

7. What decision would be best from a community perspective? Why?

8. What would you do if you were Amy Thompson? Explain the rationale for your decision from an ethical perspective.

CASE 13: A FAVOR FOR "MY FRIEND"

Since joining the North Branch School District in the early spring, new business manager Darrell Fleming had been under the microscope. His predecessor had avoided making the tough decisions when it came to transportation questions from parents and drivers. Dinah Lance, Fleming's secretary, had often been put on the spot to make decisions that were later overruled when her boss felt the pressure from the outside. Even though it was Fleming's first job as business manager, the superintendent, Dr. William Occam, had high expectations when he hired Darrell, knowing that he came well recommended for his integrity and good decision making.

Fleming began making his presence felt in a positive way by holding regular staff meetings and including other central office staff in discussions affecting the whole office. Fleming consistently sought advice from Dr. Occam on handling sensitive matters with staff, as well as appropriate ways to deal with persons in the community. On a personal note, the two shared a love for auto racing and their support for rival drivers made for a great initial icebreaker and subsequent watercooler conversations.

Having a good business manager to rely on was important for Dr. Occam, since the newly elected board members scrutinized every move the central administrators made. At the forefront of this scrutiny was Mr. Lon Surfy, who felt that his successful write-in campaign and subsequent election as board president gave him a mandate to exert influence over his fellow board members and the district staff. In the absence of a strong counterweight on the board, Dr. Occam bore the brunt of the attacks from Mr. Surfy.

Board scrutiny of expenditures on training programs for support staff was a constant sore point. The school district was not contractually obligated to pay for continuing education for the secretarial and maintenance staff, and many school board members opposed it. Another point of contention was the newly created technology manager position, which Dr. Occam had strongly advocated. The neglect in this area, combined with the technology manager's efforts to rebuild the lagging program, led to seemingly endless budgetary requests for technology upgrades.

By August of the upcoming school year, new transportation routes had been designed and the parents notified of the schedules. The transportation office received the typical requests to accommodate students moving into the district or changes in baby-sitter addresses, but for the most part the operation was normal.

As the opening week drew to a close and everyone looked forward to the first weekend of the school year, Fleming's secretary, Dinah, took a late afternoon phone call. A rather surly lady who identified herself as Mrs. Lappas demanded that her grandson's bus stop be relocated closer to her home. Dinah promised to look at it the following week.

On Monday, Dinah checked the location of the stop. It was tucked away in a new development on a relatively quiet road, and the kindergartener in question had to walk all of fifty feet to the stop. Three other students were also picked up at this stop.

Dinah knew this stop should not be relocated, but using her intuition she checked with Fleming to be sure she had covered all the bases. She prepared a chart that compared the impact on all four students of a possible change in the location of the bus stop (see table 9.1). The chart she prepared gave Fleming a confirmation of what he thought the answer would be.

That afternoon Mrs. Lappas called again and demanded to speak with the superintendent. Dinah alerted Fleming of the incoming call and the

Table 9.1. Dinah's Bus Stop Comparison

Bus: B-23		Stop 5: 26 Boone Drive		AM/PM	
Name	Address	Current Distance from Home	Changed Distance from Home	Grade	Siblings
Student A*	18 Boone Drive	50′	0′	K	No
Student B	24 Boone Drive	10′	50′	3	No
Student C	32 Boone Drive	45′	95′	K	Yes
Student D	32 Boone Drive	45′	95′	4	Yes

District policy for student walking to school/bus stop: 75 feet

*Grandson of Mrs. Lappas

request to talk with the boss. This was the cue for Fleming to get involved. He promptly took the call from Mrs. Lappas. During the course of the conversation, he learned that Mrs. Lappas cared for her grandson while her daughter and son-in-law left for work each weekday morning. She also voiced her concern that her grandson walked such a "long way" to the stop unsupervised, when the bus could easily stop at his front door. Fleming's explanation that the change would require the other three students to walk farther fell on deaf ears. The closing "revelation" from Mrs. Lappas was that her husband was a member of borough council and had many contacts on the school board.

The Dilemma

The next morning, Mr. Surfy, the board president, called and asked for a meeting with Fleming to talk about transportation procedures. This was not an unusual occurrence during the tenure of Fleming's predecessor; it was common for the board members to visit and get insight into financial reports, bill listings, and tax statements. This time, however, everyone in the central office, including Dr. Occam, knew where this was going. Mr. Surfy arrived after lunch asking for the business manager. During the meeting, Surfy was relaxed and did not refer to the matter of Mrs. Lappas and her grandson's stop. His questions were centered more on the funding formula and the contract with the transportation company. Fleming thought he had dodged the proverbial bullet. Alas, this was not to be the case; as they walked to the door leading to the parking lot, Mr. Surfy shook Fleming's hand and initiated a new topic of conversation:

Surfy: I understand Mrs. Lappas called you.
Fleming: Yes, she did; do you know her?
Surfy: Her husband and I went to school together, many years ago. Lovely people.
Fleming: Indeed.
Surfy: Listen, Darrell, I would greatly appreciate it if you took care of her request personally.
Fleming: Oh, I did already. I just wish I could have accommodated her wishes. We have a policy, as you know, about the students walking to the stops . . .

Surfy: I know that. I just think that you did not look carefully enough
           at the request my close friend made to you.

Starting to sense where this was leading, Fleming coughed nervously
and replied, "I see."

The Decision Point

Decision time for Fleming came quickly. As he released the handshake,
he promised Mr. Surfy to look at the matter one more time. What was
Fleming to do? As the board president and the leader of much of the mal-
ice toward the current administrators, Mr. Surfy certainly had the power
and wherewithal to make life miserable at the central office at best, and
direct overt attacks at Fleming and his direct-report staff at worst.

To avoid that scenario and perhaps improve his standing with Surfy
and his associates, it would make sense to approve the request to change
the bus stop. However, this one act of acquiescence would likely mean
the end of attempts to deal with all requests fairly. Make one accommo-
dation for one request for change, and the rest would follow suit. Fleming was concerned that this concession could set a precedent for future
requests from Surfy and other board members, not only in transportation but in other areas under his control as well.

Making the change was legally allowed and within the authority of the
business manager, and when viewed in isolation from the rest of the operation of the district was a minor deviation from usual practice. But in
the broader context of the role of the business manager to enforce
school district policies, whether adopted by the board or directed by
procedures, Fleming had to examine his professional responsibility and
duty. As he considered his position, he was very concerned with the implications his choice would have for the staff and their trust in their supervisor to uphold the policies and procedures of the organization in the
context of the decision-making progress.

Questions for Discussion

1. What are the legal issues in this case? Is there a legal problem?
2. What is the fairest way to handle this situation? How would Mr.
   Fleming resolve this dilemma if he were concerned about the

greatest good for the greatest number? Should that be a concern in this case? Why or why not?

3. What is the most caring way to resolve this dilemma? With respect to Mrs. Lappas? Her grandchild? The other children at bus stop number 5?

4. Who has the power in this situation? What are the different ways that various persons in this dilemma may exert their power? Is there anyone in this situation who is abusing power? Explain.

5. What impact, if any, would the various possible decisions have on the community?

6. What would the profession expect of Mr. Fleming?

7. What action would be in the best interests of the students? Explain your answer.

8. What action would you take if you were Mr. Fleming? Explain the rationale for your decision from an ethical perspective.

CASE 14: GREEN VALLEY CHRISTIAN ACADEMY

The Pine Hills School District was located in a conservative community. There was a well-organized, vocal group of citizens representing the interests of taxpayers. This group exerted considerable influence over the school at budget time, which helped keep the community's tax rate the lowest in the county.

The religious values of the residents of the school district also played a role in shaping the culture of the community. Approximately 3 percent of the families with school-age children chose to home-school their children primarily for religious reasons. Approximately 10 percent of children in the district attended church-affiliated nonpublic schools. According to state law, school districts were required to provide transportation for nonpublic students to schools within a ten-mile radius of their boundaries.

At the end of the past school year, thirty-six Pine Hills School District children were attending the Green Valley Christian Academy (GVCA). Twenty-nine of those students were from racial and ethnic minority families. Up until several years ago, about a dozen children attended this school. Then, the most efficient transportation system was to send a van to pick up children at their homes to transport them directly to the school. With the increase in the number of students, the district was re-quired to use three separate vans to transport these children to Green Valley Christian Academy. The parents of these children were very sat-isfied with the arrangements. Their children rode with their classmates in the van, and the ride times were no more than twenty-five minutes to or from the school.

As the number of students attending the school increased, a trans-portation consultant hired by the school district advised the business manager that the district could eliminate the cost of the multiple vans required to transport thirty-six students to GVCA, a $38,000 annual sav-ings to the district, by absorbing the students on a regular public school bus route. Christine Martin, the business manager, was pleased with the opportunity for meaningful savings and authorized the district's trans-portation department to implement the change for the start of the next school year.

The school board was informed about the upcoming change and the likelihood of receiving phone calls from unhappy parents. After some discussion at a board meeting, the board, attracted by the savings, sup-ported the change.

The Dilemma

The parents of the children attending GVCA were notified of the changes by letter approximately two weeks before the start of the school year. The parents immediately began calling the transportation depart-ment and the business manager to express their displeasure at the changes being implemented. The following is a sample of the comments documented from the telephone calls received from these parents:

Mrs. Jones: I don't understand why you need to make these changes. We like the service that we have been receiving. We pay taxes to the Pine Hill School District and we pay tuition to send our children to Green Valley. We don't ask for any other services from the school district except for transportation. We believe we are entitled to the level of service that we have been receiving.

Mrs. Heinz: We don't want our children to ride on the bus with public school students. We choose to send them to Green Valley Christian Academy because we do not want them to be exposed to the worldly influence of the public schools. Our children will be exposed to bad language and behavior on the bus with the public school students.

Mr. Jackson: Our children are going to be on the bus for entirely too long. The bus to Green Valley went right by our house on the way to the school. We demand that the bus stop at our house to pick up our children and drop them off. There is no reason for our children to have to ride the public school bus into the middle school to get another bus to Green Valley.

Christine Martin, in an effort to address worries and give assurances regarding the potential benefits of the new schedule, contacted each of the concerned parents personally. She asked the parents for their patience as the new system was implemented. Christine felt she had temporarily averted a substantial problem. However, she also noted that her assurances were met with no small degree of skepticism and hostility.

Believing strongly in the viability of the new system, as well as in financial rewards, the district went forward with the new system as planned at the beginning of the school year. Unfortunately, problems arose almost immediately, as clashes between the two sets of students, school bus travel time, and even charges of discrimination resulted in a second, larger round of angry calls. The following is a sample of the phone calls received during the first two weeks of school:

Mr. Griggs (GVCA parent): You are discriminating against Christian minority children. Why does it seem that only the minority students are being forced to spend extra time on the bus? Would you allow your child to ride on the bus for fifty minutes each way? I bet the public school children aren't on the bus for this long. Also, I would be willing to wager that if the students going to Green Valley were all white, they would not have to spend two hours on the buses. We demand a return to the old system of transportation. I grew up in Alabama and I recognize racism when I see it. We are taxpayers too. I have contacted the NAACP regarding this issue and their lawyers will be contacting the district.

Mrs. Richman (GVCA parent): My child has to get up too early for the bus and arrives home one hour later than he would if there were a stop by our house. A first grader is too young for this length of bus ride. He is getting sick from the length of the ride and now he doesn't want to go to school. Also, I have received a phone call from his teacher at Green Valley that he has been arriving late to school and has been using inappropriate language in class. He certainly does not learn that kind of language at home. What are you going to do about this?

Mr. Chalmers (GVCA parent): Our elementary age children have to ride on a bus with secondary students. We don't think this should be allowed. They are going to hear these older children talking about inappropriate subjects. We are contacting the State Department of Education. We have called a lawyer to represent our concerns.

Mrs. Heinz (GVCA parent): My first grade child came home from school this afternoon and started talking about sex! This is entirely inappropriate and he learned it from those kids on the bus. I warned you that this would happen and I was right. I demand that you address this issue and that our students get the same services they received last year.

Mr. Ritchie (Pine Hills School District parent): Why do you have all of those fundamentalist kids riding my daughter's bus? Our home is one of the last bus stops and by the time she gets on, there are no seats left. She has to share a seat with two other students and says that she often has difficulty finding someone who will allow her to join them. Her bus was not crowded last year. Perhaps you should hire another driver who can take over part of this bus route.

Principal Mattson (Pine Hills Middle School): We don't have staff to supervise the nonpublic students while they wait at our school for the bus that takes them home. Our bell times do not coincide with the times when they arrive and depart. If this continues, we will have to hire an additional part-time staff member in order to monitor the Green Valley students in the afternoon.

Mrs. Smith (GVCA parent): The public school children are picking on my children and making fun of their uniforms. My son got in a fight today on the bus and was punched in the mouth by another student. I would like the phone number and address of the other boy's parents so that I can confront the boy and his parents myself.

Mr. Hosterman (GVCA parent): How can you kick my son off of the school bus? He doesn't even go to your school! He was after all just defending himself from those public school bullies who make fun of his uniform every day. How is he supposed to get to Green Valley Academy now that he can no longer ride the bus? This would never have happened if you hadn't changed the existing transportation system.

Dr. Lawrence (director, Green Valley Christian Academy): The bus transporting the students from the Pine Hills School District is five minutes late every morning. All the other public school buses arrive on time. We will not continue to tolerate the late arrival of thirty-six students. Are you purposely doing this because the parents of these students have chosen to remove them from your schools? Also, I have been receiving phone calls from parents who are angry that their children are being bullied and inappropriately influenced both on the buses and while they are waiting for the arrival of the buses. You must begin to exercise proper disciplinary authority over your public school students. If this continues, we will be forced to contact the State Department of Education regarding this issue.

Mr. Johnson (Pine Hills board member): I have received five phone calls a day on this situation since the start of school, including several from the NAACP. What can we do about it? I am concerned about the length of time that these children are on the bus. Are we going to need to have our lawyers investigate this to prepare for a possible lawsuit?

The Decision Point

Christine Martin continued her beginning-of-the-year mantra for the majority of transportation complaints: "You will need to wait until we have completed the first two weeks of school before we look at making changes. Things usually tend to run longer the first few days of school, until everyone becomes more comfortable with the routine. Then we will consider making adjustments for the problems we are experiencing."

Privately Christine wondered whether the savings from the change in nonpublic transportation was worth the hassle. Would the savings be eaten up by the new costs to resolve the complaints? Should they continue to the old way of doing things with a more expensive door-to-door system that kept everyone happy?

Making this problem even worse, the school board was becoming concerned about the complaints and was pressuring for further justification for the new system. Christine Martin was informed that she would be expected to resell and further defend her decision for the transportation changes at the next school board meeting in two weeks. Should she decide to forget the new system and go back to what worked before, or should she continue the new transportation system, even in light of substantial parental discontent?

Questions for Discussion

1. What are the legal implications involved in this case?
2. What would be the fairest course of action? The most just? Are there issues of equality involved in this dilemma? If so, what are they?
3. What is the most caring approach to this dilemma?
4. Who has the power in this scenario and how is it being used? How should it be used?
5. What would the profession expect of Ms. Martin in this situation? Explain your answer.
6. What is the community's stake, if any, in this situation? How would you address community needs?
7. What actions could Ms. Martin take that would be in the best interest of the students?
8. What would you do if you were in Ms. Martin's place? What is the most ethical course of action that could be taken to resolve this dilemma? Why?

CASE OUTCOMES

This section describes the outcomes of the fourteen cases presented in part II. They are gathered in a separate chapter to assist the reader in reflecting on the ethical dilemma that is involved in each case, considering the ethical frameworks that can be used to resolve the dilemma, and formulating a solution prior to learning about the actual outcome. The outcomes are presented to provide closure to the cases; not knowing what happened can be very frustrating. However, these outcomes are not necessarily the "right" answer to the dilemma. They merely give an indication of what was ultimately done. Not all of the outcomes are positive. Some present possible mistakes the business manager made and would do differently with the benefit of hindsight. Others represent appropriate choices and innovative solutions implemented by business managers.

At the end of each outcome, there are two questions for further reflection. First, readers are asked whether they agree with the business manager's actions and then they are asked to give a rationale for their support or disagreement. Were the actions different from what they would have done under the circumstances? Second, readers are asked to reflect once again on the ethical frameworks presented in part I and to identify which framework or frameworks guided the business manager's actions. With this last step, we hope to close the circle begun in part I with the introduction of the different ethical frameworks and to have readers conclude by rethinking and broadening their point of view to encompass multiple perspectives.

CASE I: RETIREMENT BENEFITS AGREEMENT: UNDERSTANDING THE BIG PICTURE

Outcome

The business manager, Mrs. Stewart, contacted the board president informally on the telephone to "clarify the health benefit coverage for the superintendent and his wife after retirement." The president told her that the intent of the board was to provide this coverage, without specifying exactly how to do it.

Mrs. Stewart explained that the initial approach to include the superintendent in the district's self-insurance plan was inappropriate, since it would jeopardize the district's overall plan for other employees. Instead, she proposed an alternative way to achieve the same results, which the board accepted. To settle the issue, the board increased the superintendent's retirement bonus by the amount equal to the insurance premiums that he would have to pay into the plan as a retiree. This was satisfactory to the superintendent, although several board members expressed a concern that they were just providing more money, not health benefits, and that the choice of how to use the money was up to the superintendent.

Questions for Discussion

1. Do you agree with Mrs. Stewart's resolution of the problem? Why or why not?
2. What ethical frameworks do you believe she was working from in resolving this problem? Explain your reasoning.

CASE 2: TARNISHED SILVER

Outcome

John knew he had to act quickly, before Connie hurt herself irreparably by rigging the contract. He could confront her himself, but then she might take out her anger on Mary. He decided to concentrate for the moment on Doug. Who was he and what could he find out about him? Mary checked with his company and obtained his last name and home town, and passed this information on to her brother. The first thing John found out, with a simple phone call, was that Doug was married and had young children. Would this information be enough to get Connie to come down to earth?

Mary said she would take it from there. She told Connie that she had "heard through the grapevine" that Doug was married. Connie, of course, opted not to believe this. But doubts had been set up. John and Mary waited, nervously, another week. Then Connie called Mary into her office and, tearfully, said she and Doug were through and he was a thoroughgoing creep. Mary commiserated and everyone breathed a sigh of relief.

Questions for Discussion

1. Do you agree with John's resolution of the problem? Why or why not?
2. What ethical frameworks do you believe John was working from in resolving this problem? Explain your reasoning.

CASE 3: THE BLACK ROCK SCHOOL DISTRICT NEGOTIATIONS IMPASSE

Outcome

Prior to the meeting, the business manager, Mr. James, confided in Janice Davis, the superintendent, who was not involved in the original case with the teacher. He told the superintendent about the actual circumstances of the teacher's resignation and the promises of confidentiality given to the parents involved.

Following this revelation, Dr. Davis approached the union president privately and asked for a confidential discussion just between the two of them before the meeting, to which the union president agreed. The superintendent started the discussion by expressing her wish to have a fresh start in their relationship and to move forward positively. She clarified that the district had not fired Cliff, but he had chosen to resign. She provided the president with no names or details, but made it clear that he did not resign because of a teaching assignment but something much more serious.

"You don't know what went on and you never will know what went on," she said, "but I guarantee it is not something that you want to make an issue of and certainly not a strike issue. We will not discuss the events surrounding why Mr. Rankin resigned because innocent people would be hurt and we have given a promise of confidentiality to them."

Dr. Davis then assured the union president that she had her own management style and was eager to work things out on the new contract to their mutual satisfaction. She said that she was willing to resolve the remaining issues on a one-to-one basis with the union president. She concluded the discussion by emphasizing the need to move forward. "Don't keep hanging on to something I can't fix."

The gravity and resolve of the superintendent impressed the union president and he did not press her for details. With this assurance, the union president was able to go back to his members and dampen the angry feelings among his members. No strike occurred and the contract was ratified shortly thereafter.

Questions for Discussion

1. Do you agree with Mr. James's resolution of the problem? Why or why not?
2. What ethical frameworks do you believe he was working from in resolving this problem? Explain your reasoning.

CASE 4: TRAVEL EXPENSES FOR SPECIAL EDUCATION

Outcome

Jane had not met Jim before. She could immediately see why he was so well liked and why Beth (as well as everyone else) was so fond of him. As he talked, somewhat shyly, about his work with special education students, Jane thought too what charm he had and sincerity. ("He obviously cares about kids. On the other hand, are his overnight stays really due to job-related fatigue?" Jane thought to herself.) With no way to answer this last question, Jane tried another tack.

She asked Jim if he would consider working in schools closer to home, since she knew his job could be exhausting and no one wanted his safety compromised, and there was, after all, a policy about rotating itinerant teachers.

Beth stated that it was certainly not a bad idea to change Jim's schools; in fact, she was really concerned, now that he was injured.

Jim readily consented, adding that he was sure a change would be for the better.

Of course Jane approved his prior expense requests. How could she not?

Questions for Discussion

1. Do you agree with Jane's resolution of the problem? Why or why not?
2. What ethical frameworks do you believe she was working from in resolving this problem? Explain your reasoning.

CASE 5: USE OF CONSULTANTS

Outcome

"Well, you guys, it's been quite a year. Remember last time we got together I told you about not knowing what to do, with the super paying off consultants left and right, and the school board saying we shouldn't hire consultants? I thought and thought about it, and finally decided that the right thing to do was to go to Dr. Jones himself. I'd lay it on the line, tell him what I was thinking, especially since the school board had said no and I was still paying consultants. Was I wrong! He got red in the face, first, then sort of spluttered and told me I was very conscientious, but he was sure that I could bury the expenses for consultants under some other category. My mouth must have dropped open, because he said he was busy and that was that.

So what was I to do now? My wife works in a law office, and she told me that if they found out what I was doing, I could be guilty of collusion—or something like that. I was really worried. We like where we're living and my wife has a great job. No one wanted to leave, that's for sure. Anyhow, the next weekend I was at the Legion and started talking with an old guy; he was a friend of my dad's and he's been like a second father to me. I got started and the next thing you know, I was telling him my troubles, all about the consultants and everything. Darned if I forgot that his nephew was on the school board. Or maybe I didn't forget. But one thing followed another and, guess what, we have a new superintendent, and things are really looking up.

So, see you at ASBO in the fall!"

Questions for Discussion

1. Do you agree with Bob's resolution of the problem? Why or why not?
2. What ethical frameworks do you believe he was working from in resolving this problem? Explain your reasoning.

CASE 6: PURCHASING FOOTBALL EQUIPMENT

Outcome

In this instance, the business manager chose to live to fight another day. He let stand the purchase order to Sports Warehouse. However, he did use the situation to change district procedures to prevent this type of arrangement. He drafted new district purchasing policies. They were presented to the board and passed without dissent; they went into effect immediately. The new key provisions were:

1. Any firm receiving confidential information about a competitor's bid would be disqualified.
2. No personal gifts to individuals in the district were allowed. Any gift, favor, or other item with a monetary value was to be given to the district, which would then use it as appropriate. For example,

admissions to a football camp or clinic would be given to the district to decide who to send, rather than permitting a vendor to provide the free admissions directly to the coaches.

3. Any district employee who accepted a personal gift was to be disciplined. Repeated offenses could lead to dismissal.

Questions for Discussion

1. Do you agree with the business manager's resolution of the problem? Why or why not?
2. What ethical frameworks do you believe he was working from in resolving this problem? Explain your reasoning.

CASE 7: THE NEW BUSINESS MANAGER AND THE PTO TREASURER

Outcome

Maria, after some effort, scheduled a private meeting with Janet in her office. Janet was cheerful in the outer office and chatted with Sally on the way in. Maria closed the door and told Janet directly that she did not want to beat around the bush. She immediately told Janet that she had photocopied many of her records while they were in her possession and she was sure Janet was playing games with PTO funds. Also, Maria said she was "positive" that Janet had diverted funds to her personal account and she was going to go to the state police and have them subpoena her records.

Janet started to interrupt, but Maria cut her off and said, "I want you to resign your PTO treasurer's position and write the PTO a check for any money you know you have taken. If you do that, you can go on with whatever else it is that you do around here in Granite Ridge. If you do not, by the time you get in your car I will call the police to start an investigation."

Janet was visibly shaken but remained fairly composed as she replied, "Fine, I will resign but I won't promise anything about any money you think is missing." She then got up and left the office and stomped out of the building. Maria was not sure what Janet was going to do. Actually, Maria was not sure what she herself was going to do. She knew she had taken a big gamble.

The next day the principal called the superintendent and was furious that Janet had resigned not only her PTO treasurer's position but her PTO membership. The superintendent immediately called Maria into his office to tell her that he was not happy that she had met with Janet privately, and expressed his displeasure with how Maria handled this situation. He then told her that this incident reflected negatively on the school, the district, and the entire administration, including himself. He assured Maria that this would be included in her evaluation. Two days later, Maria learned from the superintendent that Janet had made a $3,250 donation for the new playground equipment at the school.

Questions for Discussion

1. Do you agree with Maria's resolution of the problem? Why or why not?
2. What ethical frameworks do you believe she was working from in resolving this problem? Explain your reasoning.

CASE 8: SUPPORT YOUR LOCAL BANK

Outcome

Susan realized that being rigid and adamant was counterproductive. Taking her revised analysis to the superintendent, she asked whether they could find ways to work with Alpha Bank. If the local bank knew of its uncompetitive position, could it expand and improve its services to help the district get what it needed in this area? In fact, she stressed, it could be to Alpha's benefit to learn how far ahead in the marketplace its competitors were.

The superintendent agreed to an informal meeting with the top officers of Alpha Bank to share their findings. During the meeting, he made it clear the school district was not contemplating changing banks but wanted to discuss future possible improvements in their existing relationship. He also made Susan's point to the bank officers that knowing what their competitors were offering could help Alpha stay abreast of the current market environment and avoid difficulties with other clients.

Questions for Discussion

1. Do you agree with Susan's resolution of the problem? Why or why not?
2. What ethical frameworks do you believe she was working from in resolving this problem? Explain your reasoning.

CASE 9: INVESTMENT ADVISERS

Outcome

Ms. Zoltek decided to go back to Dr. Mariwell and plead her position, emphasizing how wrong it would be to go with GFG. However, he dismissed her concerns out of hand and lectured her about decision making and how choices can extend beyond simple factual data.

At the school board meeting, the superintendent recommended to the board that GFG be retained as the district's financial adviser, and the board approved the arrangement without delving into the fact that the district would be paying a higher price.

Ms. Zoltek was dismayed by what she saw as blatant cronyism. This incident was the most obvious example but was also indicative of many other questionable smaller actions of the district management team, particularly the superintendent. These cumulative events jaded her against public school business management. After another year and a half in the district, she decided to change her career track and seek employment outside of education. Dr. Mariwell remained at the district for another nine years, after which he retired and took on consulting assignments with various school districts and related entities.

Questions for Discussion

1. Do you agree with Ms. Zoltek's resolution of the problem? Why or why not?

2. What ethical frameworks do you believe she was working from in resolving this problem? Explain your reasoning.

CASE 10: THE HISTORIC SCHOOL

Outcome

The business manager realized that the fate of Fairview School was a sensitive issue to the community. After touring the school and listening to the testimony at the school board meeting, he was convinced that it was important to save Fairview, in fact to restore it.

As he wrote his report recommending either the alternative high school proposal or the equally preservation-oriented library proposal, his concern was to make his decision palatable to the school board. He posed this question: Would saving the school offset the potential loss in revenue gained by selling the site to a developer? That is, would ill will toward the district for manifesting what could very well be viewed as a callous lack of community spirit have repercussions later, when the district wanted community support and involvement? If a tax increase turned out to be unavoidable, was it not important to have this support?

To further bolster his position, he found several historic preservation grant possibilities and websites devoted to adaptive reuse of historic structures. These told about success stories for other old buildings, with gains to the community as a result. He included this information in the report, added the city zoning officer's caveat about the difficulty of making changes in zoning laws, hoped it wasn't too heavy-handed, and submitted it.

The next board meeting was even more crowded with Fairview supporters. Although there were some grumbling remarks by the taxpayers group, the mood was jubilant when the report recommended saving the school. The board subsequently made the decision to go with the alternative high school proposal, and the district was successful in receiving two grants for interior and exterior renovations.

At the grand opening of the renovated school, an honored guest was one of the artists who, as a young man, had worked on the mural. The following year, Fairview Alternative School won a state historic preservation award.

Questions for Discussion

1. Do you agree with the SBO's decision? Why or why not?
2. How would you deal with the grumbling taxpayers?
3. From an ethical perspective, would it influence your decision if you knew that the building might qualify for an award?

CASE 11: SOFTWARE OWNERSHIP

Outcome

After more discussion among the three administrators, the district decided to establish an ownership agreement with Curtis. This was counter to the initial inclination of the business manager, but he agreed after considering the full range of concerns involved. The main features of the agreement were:

1. The technology coordinator and the district would have joint ownership of FUS software.
2. The district would have unrestricted use of the FUS software.
3. The technology coordinator would receive all revenue from FUS software sales and installation. The district would not receive any of these revenues.
4. The technology coordinator would assume full ownership of the FUS software if he left the district, but the district would retain the right to use it.

At first glance, the district surrendered an important principle by recognizing the technology coordinator's ownership rights to a product that was developed with district assistance and (possibly) on district time. However, in the final analysis more pragmatic reasons motivated the district's action. First, the district did not want to lose Curtis over this issue. His services to the district were important and would not be easily replaced. Second, the revenue issue was negated when district administrators found out that the revenues involved were nominal; they were primarily to cover the technology coordinator's expenses for installation and training and did not represent a significant revenue loss to the district. Finally, the business manager and other administrators were motivated by the prevailing norm of sharing good ideas and practices among surrounding districts.

The technology coordinator was pleased with the agreement and signed it. For him it represented fair treatment for his extra work outside the district and recognition by the district of the value of his work for them. He is still employed by the district.

Questions for Discussion

1. Do you agree with the district's resolution of the problem? Why or why not?
2. What ethical frameworks do you believe the district was working from in resolving this problem? Explain your reasoning.

CASE 12: SPECIAL BUS STOP

Outcome

Within one week of their initial phone conversation, Mrs. Thompson called Mr. Starner to share the results of her investigation. She informed him that the original decision of the transportation coordinator would be upheld. As expected, the ensuing conversation did not go well. Mr. Starner asked Mrs. Thompson who would be responsible in the event that something happened to his granddaughter as she was walking to school and warned her that his son's lawyer was perfectly willing to "go to war" for a second time against a recalcitrant school district. Mrs. Thompson chose her response carefully, but ultimately advised Mr. Starner that it is a parent's prerogative to take steps to ensure his or her child's safety. The conversation concluded with Mr. Starner requesting to speak to the superintendent and threatening to contact the members of the school board and the media.

Several weeks passed after Mr. Starner's threats to challenge her decision and nothing happened. Neither the superintendent nor the board called her in to justify her denial of the special bus stop. Nothing appeared in the local paper. The remainder of the year passed without further contact from Mr. Starner.

Questions for Discussion

1. Do you agree with Mrs. Thompson's resolution of the problem? Why or why not?
2. What ethical frameworks do you believe she was working from in resolving this problem? Explain your reasoning.

CASE 13: A FAVOR FOR "MY FRIEND"

Outcome

The truth was that Darrell Fleming had made up his mind even as he returned to his office after leaving Mr. Surfy. Although he weighed the pros and cons of his choice, he knew exactly how he was going to respond to Mr. Surfy's not-so-veiled threat. This was his first job, he thought he might well be on shaky ground, and he felt he did not have the experience to challenge Mr. Surfy's power. He phoned Mrs. Lappas immediately and told her that he would change the bus route to pick up her grandson at her door beginning next week. He then called Dinah and told her to adjust the bus route to accommodate Mrs. Lappas's request.

Questions for Discussion

1. Do you agree with Darrell's resolution of the problem? Why or why not?
2. What ethical frameworks do you believe he was working from in resolving this problem? Explain your reasoning.

CASE 14: GREEN VALLEY CHRISTIAN ACADEMY

Outcome

Christine Martin decided to focus on resolving the most prominent complaints in order to buy time to allow the other parents and students from both the Pine Hills School District and the Green Valley Christian Academy to adjust to and accept the new system. She called in the district's transportation coordinator and the transportation consultant who had recommended the new system. The three of them met to deal with the major problems. Tinkering with the schedules and stops, they were able to reduce the longest ride times, particularly for younger children. Elementary and secondary students were largely, but not entirely, served on different buses. Students now arrived at GVCA on time, and the new schedule was coordinated with the middle school timetable so that students were not left unsupervised.

A separate educational initiative was put into place to eliminate harassment and bullying on the buses. This included a brief period of employing bus monitors to ride the two buses where the problem was most prevalent. The presence of a bus monitor was effective and no further incidents occurred, even after the use of monitors was discontinued.

These efforts paid off and the complaint level was reduced. Ms. Martin reported the early results at the next board meeting and promised to resolve remaining complaints. As a result, the board agreed to maintain the new busing system and did not add more vans or buses to transport the non–public school children. As the school year progressed, the transportation coordinator made additional adjustments to the system to improve the bus service.

Questions for Discussion

1. Do you agree with Ms. Martin's resolution of the problem? Why or why not?
2. What ethical frameworks do you believe she was working from in resolving this problem? Explain your reasoning.

REFERENCES

Apple, M. W. 2003. *The State and the Politics of Knowledge*. New York: Routledge Falmer.

———. 2001. *Educating the "Right" Way: Markets, Standards, God, and Inequality*. New York: Routledge Falmer.

Association of School Business Officials International. 2001. *Professional Standards*. Reston, VA: Association of School Business Officials International.

Begley, P. T., and J. A. Stefkovich, eds. "Education, Ethics, and the 'Cult of Efficiency': Implications for Values and Leadership." 2004. *Journal of Educational Administration* 42, no. 2.

Furman, G. C. 2003. "The Ethic of Community." *Journal of Educational Administration* 42, no. 2: 215–35.

Hartman, W. T. 1999. *School District Budgeting*. Reston, VA: Association of School Business Officials International.

No Child Left Behind Act of 2001. 20 U.S.C. 6301 et seq. 2002.

Noddings, N. 2003. *Caring: A Feminine Approach to Ethics and Moral Education*. 2nd ed. Berkeley: University of California Press.

———. 1992. *The Challenge to Care in Schools: An Alternative Approach to Education*. New York: Teachers College Press.

Sergiovanni, T. J. 1994. *Building Community in Schools*. San Francisco: Jossey-Bass.

Sernak, K. 1998. *School Leadership: Balancing Power with Caring*. New York: Teachers College Press.

Shapiro, J., and J. A. Stefkovich. 2001. *Ethical Leadership and Decision Making in Education*. Mahwah, NJ: Lawrence Erlbaum.

Starratt, R. J. 1994. *Building an Ethical School*. London: Falmer.

Stefkovich, J. A., and G. M. O'Brien. 2004. "Best Interests of the Student: An Ethical Model." *Journal of Educational Administration* 42, no. 2: 197–214.

Strike, K. A., E. J. Haller, and J. F. Soltis. 1998. *The Ethics of School Administration*. 2nd ed. New York: Teachers College Press.

INDEX

ABOUT THE AUTHORS

William T. Hartman is a professor of education in the College of Education at Pennsylvania State University and cofounder and the executive director of the Center for Total Quality Schools at Penn State. He was a recipient of the Graduate Faculty Teaching Award for the University for 1999. Prior to coming to Penn State in 1986, he was on the faculty at the University of Oregon and Stanford University. He has served on the board of directors of the American Education Finance Association, and was a visiting fellow in education at the University of Sussex (United Kingdom) in 1994 and at Cambridge University in 2003.

Dr. Hartman has a bachelor of mechanical engineering with high honors from the University of Florida, a master's of business administration from Harvard University, and a Ph.D. in administration and policy analysis from Stanford University. His areas of research include school budgeting, special education finance, school finance equity, resource allocation at the school and district levels, total quality management in education, and microcomputer models in educational administration. He is a frequent contributor to professional journals in these fields. He has served as a consultant to various educational agencies at the federal, state, and local levels, to research organizations, to private industry, and to special interest groups in education. His latest books are

School District Budgeting and *Resource Allocation and Productivity in Education.*

Jacqueline A. Stefkovich is a professor of educational administration and head of the Department of Education Policy Studies at The Pennsylvania State University, where she teaches courses related to ethics, school law and personnel administration. She holds a doctoral degree in administration, planning, and social policy from Harvard University's Graduate School of Education and a J.D. from the University of Pennsylvania Law School. She began her professional career as a teacher and public school guidance counselor and is licensed to practice law in New Jersey, Pennsylvania, and the District of Columbia.

Dr. Stefkovich's research interests focus on ethics in school leadership and students' constitutional rights, namely, the Fourth Amendment in public schools (search and seizure). With Joan Shapiro, she has written and conducted research on ethical decision making for educational leaders. Their book, *Ethical Leadership and Decision Making in Education: Applying Theoretical Perspectives to Complex Dilemmas*, was based on nine years of collaborative teaching and research in this area. Dr. Stefkovich serves on several editorial boards and has published extensively in peer-reviewed journals. She has also contributed to *School Business Affairs* and the *ASBO Legal Handbook* and has conducted workshops on ethics for school business officials.